P9-DNM-688

DISCARD

New Tecumseth Public Library

Seven Wonders of
SPACE
TECHNOLOGY

Fred Bortz

Twenty-First Century Books

Minneapolis

*For readers whose imaginations
are too vast for this small planet*

Copyright © 2011 by Alfred B. Bortz

All rights reserved. International copyright secured. No part of this book may be reproduced, stored in a retrieval system, or transmitted in any form or by any means—electronic, mechanical, photocopying, recording, or otherwise—without the prior written permission of Lerner Publishing Group, Inc., except for the inclusion of brief quotations in an acknowledged review.

Twenty-First Century Books
A division of Lerner Publishing Group, Inc.
241 First Avenue North
Minneapolis, MN 55401 U.S.A.

Website address: www.lernerbooks.com

Library of Congress Cataloging-in-Publication Data

Bortz, Fred.
     Seven wonders of space technology / by Fred Bortz.
        p.   cm. – (Seven wonders)
     Includes bibliographical references and index.
     ISBN 978–0–7613–5453–6 (lib. bdg. : alk. paper)
     1. Astronautics—Juvenile literature. 2. Space vehicles—Juvenile literature. 3. Outer space—Exploration—Juvenile literature. I. Title.
     TL793.B665 2011
     629.4—dc22   2010023996

Manufactured in the United States of America
1 – DP – 12/31/10

Contents

INTRODUCTION

*P*EOPLE LOVE TO MAKE LISTS OF THE BIGGEST AND THE BEST. ALMOST TWENTY-FIVE HUNDRED YEARS AGO, A GREEK WRITER NAMED HERODOTUS MADE A LIST OF THE MOST AWESOME THINGS EVER BUILT BY PEOPLE. THE LIST INCLUDED BUILDINGS, STATUES, AND OTHER OBJECTS THAT WERE LARGE, WONDROUS, AND IMPRESSIVE. LATER, OTHER WRITERS ADDED NEW ITEMS TO THE LIST. WRITERS EVENTUALLY AGREED ON A FINAL LIST. IT WAS CALLED THE SEVEN WONDERS OF THE ANCIENT WORLD.

The list became so famous that people began imitating it. They made other lists of wonders. They listed the Seven Wonders of the Modern World and the Seven Wonders of the Middle Ages.

People even made lists of the wonders of the universe. Those lists included dazzling and sometimes mysterious objects that shine in the sky. Long ago it was enough for people to gaze in awe at those wonders. But now modern scientists want to understand the wonders. They want to measure them. They want to touch them with machines and tools if not with their hands.

Measuring instruments, machines, and tools are technology. Those human inventions are often as wondrous as the space objects they are designed to study.

Choosing seven of those wonders for this book is not the same as choosing the seven wonders of space technology. We know that by selecting only seven, we are leaving out hundreds of other remarkable tools and machines used to explore the secrets of the universe.

WONDERFUL TOOLS OF DISCOVERY

We chose our seven examples because they explore the great questions that people ask about Earth, the solar system, and the universe. They are among the most remarkable technologies that people have ever designed and built.

We begin with telescopes called the Great Observatories. These wonders orbit, or circle, Earth. They peer into the universe with technological eyes, detecting light that is too faint for our eyes to see. They detect energy that we cannot sense—energy that tells the story of the powerful events that shape the universe.

Many countries are working together on the International Space Station (below).

We then visit the International Space Station. That orbiting laboratory is being built by twenty-six nations. Next, we discover artificial satellites that measure Earth in ways that would be impossible from the ground.

We then turn to space probes that visit other worlds. Our first destination is the Moon, where humans may soon land for the first time in fifty years. We also crawl with robot geologists across the surface of Mars, looking for signs of past or present life. Then we follow a spacecraft to the distant, frigid region of the solar system called Kuiper Belt. Its first destination there will be the dwarf planet Pluto and its moons.

Finally, we look ahead to rockets of the future. They will speed up travel within the solar system. Someday they may even carry space probes to explore the planets of other stars.

1 THE GREAT Observatories

Stars in the night sky have
fascinated humans for centuries.

*A*STRONOMY IS HUMANITY'S OLDEST SCIENCE. PEOPLE HAVE STUDIED THE NIGHT SKY FOR THOUSANDS OF YEARS. ANCIENT MONUMENTS SUCH AS STONEHENGE IN ENGLAND OR CHICHÉN ITZÁ IN MEXICO WERE PROBABLY THE GREAT OBSERVATORIES OF THEIR TIME.

Over the centuries, humans have built many other great observatories. Each one used the greatest technologies available. Each one changed the way we view our place in the universe.

But one technology changed astronomy more than any other—the ability to launch scientific equipment into space. Some of our greatest modern astronomical discoveries come from instruments that scientists have sent into orbit around or near Earth. The U.S. National Aeronautics and Space Administration (NASA) grouped four of those into one program named the Great Observatories.

Stonehenge in England is thought to be an ancient observatory.

DISCOVERING OUR PLACE IN THE UNIVERSE

Ancient civilizations saw the universe very differently than we do. To them, Earth was completely separate from what they called the heavens. They didn't think of Earth as a planet. They saw our world as the center of the universe. They believed that the Sun, the Moon, the planets, and the stars traveled around Earth.

Over the centuries, our understanding of the universe changed. We know that eight planets, including Earth, orbit the Sun. Many smaller bodies also orbit the Sun (including moons that orbit the planets). Those bodies, the planets, and the Sun make up the solar system.

We know that the Sun is slightly larger than the average star. It is one of hundreds of billions that make up a system of stars called the Milky Way Galaxy.

We know that the Milky Way is one galaxy among trillions spread out in every direction. The universe is so large that the light from the nearest galaxy takes 2.5 million years to reach us. The most distant galaxies are so far away that we see their light billions of years after it was produced.

In 1609 Italian astronomer Galileo Galilei (below) was the first person to look at the Moon through a telescope.

All of that knowledge came from telescopes on Earth. Attached to those telescopes are devices that break up the light into its mix of many colors. That mix is called a spectrum (*pl.* spectra). The instruments that break up the light and study its colors are called spectroscopes. The spectra of stars tell us what they are made of and how they produce their light and heat. The spectra of galaxies tell us that the universe is expanding. It's moving outward as if it was produced in a giant explosion.

WHY PUT OBSERVATORIES IN SPACE?

We can learn so much from telescopes on the ground. So why are we sending telescopes into space? The answer begins with a simple twinkle.

Most people love to see the twinkling of the stars on a clear night. But astronomers know that stars don't really twinkle. Stars put out a steady stream of light.

That starlight's path bends a little bit as it passes through Earth's atmosphere (the layer of gases surrounding the planet). The temperature and pressure of the atmosphere, or air, changes. As it changes, so does the amount of light bending. Those changes produce the twinkling we see. Air changes also make telescope images less sharp. Putting a telescope above Earth's atmosphere gets rid of that problem.

The atmosphere affects our observations in other ways. Light is a form of energy called an electromagnetic wave. Electromagnetic waves travel through space as a back-and-forth pulsing of electricity and magnetism. Like waves on the ocean, they have peaks and valleys. The space between two peaks is called a wavelength.

Humans see different wavelengths of light as different colors. The range of light we can see is called the visible spectrum. Red light has the longest wavelength of all visible colors. Violet light has the shortest.

Visible light is only one part of a broader electromagnetic spectrum. Beyond the colors we see are other forms of electromagnetic waves. On the long wavelength end, just beyond red, is infrared light. Then come microwaves and radio waves. On the short wavelength end, past blue and violet, is ultraviolet

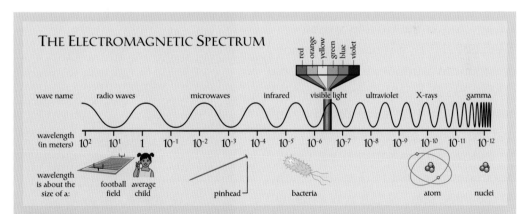

This diagram shows the electromagnetic spectrum. The spectrum includes visible light, which humans see as colors. The images at the bottom show that some waves are as long as a football field. Others are so short that they are smaller than atoms (tiny particles of matter).

(UV) light. The wavelengths of X-rays and gamma rays are even shorter.

Earth's atmosphere allows visible light to pass through. But it blocks some longer and shorter electromagnetic waves. Putting a telescope in orbit around Earth beyond the atmosphere avoids that blockage.

Space telescopes are orbiting observatories. Their telescopes capture light with mirrors, lenses, or other devices. That light includes the infrared and UV light blocked by Earth's atmosphere. Space telescopes also carry spectroscopes and other instruments to study what they detect.

Infrared, UV, and visible light spectra tell astronomers what stars are made of. They tell astronomers which chemical substances are present in stars—and how much. They reveal what gases make up a planet's atmosphere. Infrared spectra can also be used to measure temperature patterns on planets and moons.

The more wavelengths we can detect, the more we can learn about the objects we are viewing. That simple fact led NASA to plan, build, and launch its Great Observatories into space.

THE HUBBLE SPACE TELESCOPE

The first and most famous Great Observatory is the Hubble Space Telescope (HST). It is named in honor of American astronomer Edwin Hubble (1889–1953). Hubble first discovered galaxies in the 1920s. He also discovered that the universe is expanding.

NASA astronomers and engineers began designing the HST in the 1970s. At the same time, NASA was working on space shuttles to carry people and heavy loads into space. So NASA designed the HST to be launched by a space shuttle. Once in orbit, the HST

Astronomer Edwin Hubble looks through the eyepiece of a giant telescope at the Mount Wilson Observatory in California in 1937.

The Hubble Space Telescope orbits above Earth.

would be serviced by space shuttle astronauts. The astronauts would adjust, repair, and replace HST equipment and instruments.

At first, NASA hoped to launch the HST in 1983. But designing and building it took longer than expected. Then, on January 28, 1986, the space shuttle *Challenger* exploded soon after takeoff. All seven crew members were killed. The space shuttle program came to a halt while engineers worked to figure out what had gone wrong with *Challenger*.

The HST was finally launched and reached orbit in April 1990. But that wasn't the end of its troubles. The images the HST was sending back to Earth were not nearly as sharp as astronomers expected.

What was causing the blurring? Scientists soon realized that the problem was Hubble's mirror. It had been made precisely—but it was the wrong shape! To fix the problem, NASA needed to design and build two large new pieces of technology.

One was a new camera called the Wide Field and Planetary Camera 2 (WFPC2). WFPC2 was about as large as a baby grand piano. It had a built-in correction for the misshaped mirror. The other technology was a set of mirrors in a box about the size of a bathroom shower stall. NASA called it COSTAR. That stands for Corrective Optics Space Telescope Axial Replacement.

WFPC2 and COSTAR were installed on the first Hubble servicing mission in 1993. The work was a great success. The HST began sending amazing images of outer space back to Earth.

In May 2009, the fourth and final HST servicing mission took place. Astronauts added, repaired, or replaced many major parts of the observatory. Those included WFPC2, COSTAR, other cameras, spectroscopes, and other instruments. The upgraded HST immediately started sending back better pictures than ever before.

In time, the HST's instruments and computers will stop working. But if the repairs last as long as planned, the HST will continue to send images and data back to Earth until about 2014.

ON *Display*

On the final HST servicing mission in 2009, astronauts replaced WFPC2 and COSTAR. Both were brought back to Earth. They are on permanent exhibit in the Smithsonian's National Air and Space Museum in Washington, D.C.

Hubble's WFPC2 took this photo of the Crab Nebula. The nebula is what's left of a star that has exploded.

THE COMPTON GAMMA RAY OBSERVATORY

The HST detects visible light, infrared light, and UV light. The other Great Observatories observe the universe in different parts of the electromagnetic spectrum. Each part of the spectrum gives astronomers different information about the bodies of the solar system, other stars and galaxies, and the universe itself.

The second of the Great Observatories launched was the Compton Gamma Ray Observatory (CGRO). It was designed to detect gamma rays. Gamma rays are at the shortest wavelength (or highest energy) end of the electromagnetic spectrum.

Space shuttle *Atlantis* carried the CGRO into orbit in 1991. It weighed 37,000 pounds (17,000 kilograms). At that time, it was the heaviest rocket load of space science equipment ever launched.

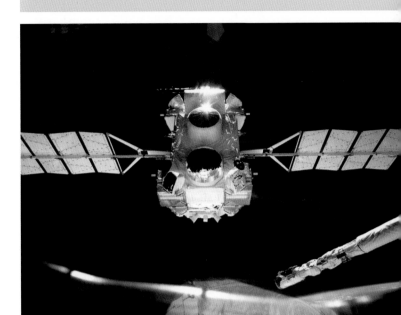

This photo shows the Compton Gamma Ray Observatory being released from the space shuttle Atlantis in 1991.

The CGRO is named in honor of Arthur Holly Compton (1892–1962). In the 1920s, Compton made important discoveries about how gamma rays behave.

Gamma rays are produced in large numbers on Earth when a nuclear bomb explodes. In the 1960s, the U.S. military put gamma ray detectors into orbit. Scientists used the detectors to look for signs that other countries were secretly testing nuclear weapons. To their

GAMMA RAYS *from the Moon*

CGRO images show that the Moon gives off gamma rays. They are produced when high-energy particles from the Sun strike the Moon. That effect is similar to the way X-ray machines produce their radiation.

The Great Observatories

13

surprise, the scientists also found gamma ray bursts (GRBs). The GRBs were coming from beyond the Milky Way Galaxy.

Astronomers knew that something powerful was happening in outer space to produce those gamma rays. But what was it? Astronomers thought colliding or exploding stars might be producing the rays. But they needed new observations to test their ideas.

CGRO was designed to make those observations. It had instruments to detect and measure GRBs and other sources of gamma rays in space.

The measurements revealed that most GRBs release a huge amount of energy. They put out as much energy in a few seconds as the Sun will produce in its entire lifetime. But GRBs are very rare. In any single galaxy, a GRB probably takes place less than once in a few billion years. That's good news for humans. Scientists think that a GRB anywhere in the Milky Way Galaxy would produce gamma rays strong enough to wipe out most life on Earth.

In November 1999, one the CGRO's gyroscopes failed. A gyroscope is a device that points an instrument in the right direction. The CGRO could still operate normally. But NASA knew that they would lose control of the CGRO if a second gyroscope went bad.

Without control, the CGRO might crash to Earth in the wrong place. Some large pieces might not burn up in the atmosphere. If the pieces fell on cities or towns, they could cause a lot of damage or injury.

Rather than risk that, NASA decided to crash the CGRO on purpose. NASA crashed the observatory into the Pacific Ocean on June 4, 2000. The Fermi Gamma Ray Space Telescope replaced it in 2008.

THE END OF A *Great Observatory*

What will happen to Hubble when it stops working? NASA's original plan was to bring it back by space shuttle and put it on display. But the HST will probably still be working when the shuttle fleet is retired (probably in 2011). So Hubble's end will probably be similar to the CGRO's.

During the final HST service mission, astronauts attached a Soft Capture and Rendezvous System (SCRS). When the time comes, a robot spacecraft will attach an engine to the SCRS. The engine will send the Hubble on a final controlled plunge toward Earth.

THE CHANDRA X-RAY OBSERVATORY

NASA launched the third of the Great Observatories, the Chandra X-ray Observatory, in 1999. To look at X-rays from space, Chandra has to orbit about 40,000 miles (64,000 kilometers) above Earth's surface.

Chandra's orbit is a long oval. At its closest point, Chandra is 9,900 miles (16,000 km) from Earth. At its farthest point, it is 83,000 miles (133,000 km) away. That's more than one-third of the way to the Moon!

Chandra was named in honor of Subrahmanyan Chandrasekhar (1910–1995). Chandrasekhar was an Indian-born American physicist. He is best known for his studies in the 1930s and 1940s of how stars evolve.

A star produces energy by a process called nuclear fusion. During fusion, the nucleus (or central portion) of one atom joins (fuses) with another. That

The Chandra X-ray Observatory (inside the white metal container, center) *is lifted up to be installed on the space shuttle* Columbia (right). *Chandra and* Columbia *lifted off on June 24, 1999.*

forms a nucleus of a different kind. Over time, most of the star's nuclei change to the new type. Then those new nuclei begin to fuse. The star changes form and enters a new stage of life.

A star may pass through several stages. Each stage is marked by a different kind of fusion. Finally, it reaches the point where no more fusion can take place, and the star begins to die.

A small star may end its life as a hot cinder called a white dwarf. White dwarf stars no longer produce energy by fusion. But they are so hot that they glow brightly for many billions of years.

Heavier stars die in giant explosions called supernovas. After the explosion, all that remains is a core. The cores of the largest supernovas pack a lot of matter into a small space. That gives them a very strong gravitational pull. Not even light can escape the gravity. Such cores are called black holes.

But if the supernova is not too large, its remaining matter becomes a neutron star. Neutron stars give off powerful beams of electromagnetic energy. They also spin quite fast. Each time the spinning beam points in Earth's direction, astronomers detect a short pulse of radio waves. So they see the star as a steadily pulsing object that they call a pulsar.

HOW THE *Sun Will Die*

In about five billion years, the Sun will enter a new stage of life. It will become a red giant star. Its central core will become much smaller and hotter. But its outer layers will swell up like a balloon and get cooler (but still red hot). The Sun will then be about as large as Earth's orbit. Its heat will destroy all life on Earth. It might even burn up the planet. About one billion years after that, the Sun will run out of fuel. Its red giant stage will end. It will end its life as a slowly cooling white dwarf about the size of Earth.

"The Great Observatories program . . . shows how astronomers need as many tools as possible to tackle the big questions out there."
—NASA's Ed Weiler, 2009, on the tenth anniversary of Chandra's launch

This illustration made from images taken by the Chandra X-ray Observatory shows a black hole. The illustration was created in 2003.

Studying pulsars is one important use of the Chandra X-ray Observatory. When scientists look at Chandra's images of a pulsar, they see a glow of X-rays. The X-rays tell them what happened to the outer portions of the dying star after the supernova explosion. And that helps them better understand the explosion itself.

Chandra is also useful for studying black holes of all sizes. Black holes can't be seen directly. But they heat up the matter that is swirling around them. That matter gets so hot that it glows at X-ray wavelengths.

Every galaxy has an extremely large, or supermassive, black hole at its center. Supermassive black holes are millions of times heavier than our Sun. But other black holes weigh only as much as some large stars. How large?

Scientists are still looking for that answer. It is fitting that a great observatory named for Chandrasekhar may provide the evidence they need.

THE SPITZER SPACE TELESCOPE

The last of the Great Observatories is the Spitzer Space Telescope. NASA launched it in August 2003. It observes the universe in infrared light. Its name honors American astronomer Lyman Spitzer (1914–1997).

A warm object such as Earth gives off heat waves in the form of infrared light. To avoid Earth's infrared glow, the Spitzer was launched into an Earth-trailing orbit. It follows the same path as Earth around the Sun but about a month behind. It is aimed away from Earth and has a reflective shield to block the Sun.

On Earth, infrared telescopes are chilled with the coldest liquid known—liquid helium. Helium cools a telescope so that its own heat doesn't overwhelm the dim infrared light it is trying to detect.

The Spitzer carried four infrared instruments into space. Engineers working on the project knew the chill of outer space would be enough to cool two of the instruments. But the other two would need liquid helium coolant. Those two were built to detect infrared light with the longest wavelengths.

The engineers knew the Spitzer couldn't have an unlimited supply of liquid helium. The rockets that launched the Spitzer into orbit could only handle a

This drawing shows the Spitzer Space Telescope in orbit. NASA launched the Spitzer in 2003.

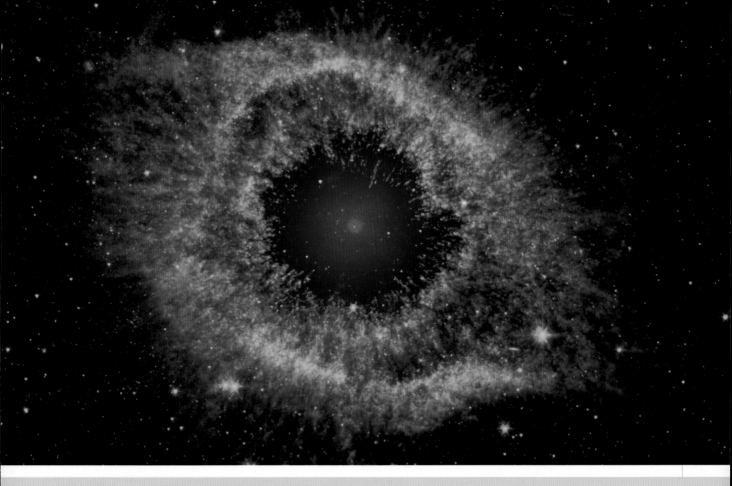

This image was taken by the Spitzer Space Telescope in 2007. It shows the Helix Nebula in the constellation Aquarius. This nebula is called a planetary nebula and is the remains of a star similar to Earth's Sun.

certain amount of weight. More liquid helium meant fewer instruments. More instruments meant less liquid helium. The Spitzer engineers had to find a balance.

The engineers finally settled on enough liquid helium to last five years. The Spitzer ran out of coolant in early 2009. Its two long-wavelength instruments stopped working. But its two shorter-wavelength instruments continue to work well. They study objects as close as near-Earth asteroids and as far away as the most distant galaxies.

Perhaps most exciting is what those detectors may tell us about planets orbiting other stars. NASA and the European Space Agency (ESA) have launched planet-hunting missions. They are looking for Earthlike worlds around other stars. As those worlds are found, the Spitzer will be able to study their atmospheres. If the Spitzer's instruments detect oxygen, that would be a strong sign of life on other worlds.

2 THE INTERNATIONAL
Space Station

*The International Space
Station orbits above Earth.*

$\mathscr{T}$HE SOVIET UNION (USSR) LAUNCHED THE WORLD'S FIRST ARTIFICIAL SATELLITE IN OCTOBER 1957. IT WAS CALLED *SPUTNIK 1*. THE UNITED STATES WAS ALARMED BY THE EVENT. THE USSR AND THE UNITED STATES—THE WORLD'S GREAT SUPERPOWERS AT THE TIME—WERE RACING TO BUILD STRONGER WEAPONS AND BETTER SPY TECHNOLOGY TO USE AGAINST EACH OTHER. WITH THE LAUNCH OF *SPUTNIK*, IT SEEMED THAT THE USSR WAS WINNING THE TECHNOLOGY RACE. THE UNITED STATES WANTED TO CATCH UP.

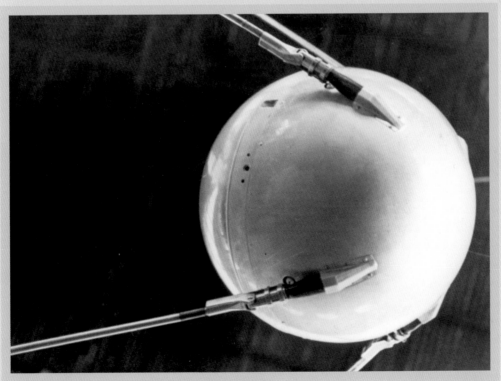

The Soviet Union launched Sputnik 1 *in 1957.*

In 1958 the United States created its space agency, NASA. In April 1961, the USSR sent the first human into orbit. A month later, U.S. president John F. Kennedy set a goal for NASA to send astronauts to the Moon by the end of the 1960s. NASA immediately began working to meet that goal.

NASA succeeded with the Apollo program. Six times between July 1969 and December 1972, Apollo spacecraft landed on the Moon's surface. Apollo astronauts explored the surface and collected rock and soil samples. Then they returned to Earth.

The United States had won the race to the Moon. Yet many scientists and engineers looked beyond this competition. They asked a different question. If one nation alone had made such a great technological advance, what could nations achieve together?

The final Apollo mission in 1975 began to answer that question. That mission didn't send astronauts to the Moon. Instead, it carried them to meet Soviet cosmonauts in a Soyuz spacecraft. For forty-four hours, the two spacecraft were joined. Their crews exchanged flags and gifts. They carried out scientific experiments together.

International competition still drives the space programs of many nations. But Apollo-Soyuz established a spirit of cooperation. That spirit has led to a truly great wonder of space technology—the International Space Station (ISS). This laboratory orbits Earth about 200 miles (320 km) above the ground. It is the largest and most expensive artificial satellite in history.

The Apollo-Soyuz crew in 1975, from left to right: American astronauts Deke Slayton, Tom Stafford, Vance Brand, and Russian cosmonauts Aleksey Leonov and Valeriy Kubasov. The model in front of the crew shows the Apollo and Soyuz spacecrafts joined together.

The space shuttle Endeavour *approaches Zarya (background), the first section of the ISS, in 1998. The shuttle crew delivered and attached Unity, the second ISS section, to Zarya.*

A CONSTRUCTION PROJECT IN ORBIT

The ISS was not built on Earth and launched into space. It is much too large. One rocket could not have carried it into orbit. And it is so expensive that no single country's space agency could afford to build it.

The ISS was put together one section, or module, at a time. Many countries have given funds, equipment, and workers to the project.

Russia launched the first unit on November 20, 1998. It is called Zarya (Russian for "sunrise"). Zarya's main body was a cylinder 13.5 feet (4.1 meters) around and 41.2 feet (12.6 m) long. Attached to that was a solar panel 35 feet (10.7 m) long and 11 feet (3.4 m) wide. The panel absorbs sunlight to produce electricity. Zarya also had rockets to adjust its orbit, a guidance system to control the direction it points in space, and storage areas. Altogether, it weighed 42,600 pounds (19,300 kg), about as much as a typical heavy truck on the highway. It had most of what was needed to start a space construction project.

Space shuttle *Endeavour* delivered the second module two weeks later. It was a node, or connecting unit. It gave the United States a place to attach its sections of the ISS to the Russian sections. It was appropriately called Unity.

On July 12, 2000, Russia launched a service module, Zvezda (star). It is

"It's amazing; as you fly over the world, you look down and you wonder why we squabble over lines between countries."

—ISS commander Kenneth D. Bowersox, 2003

slightly smaller than Zarya. It carried communications equipment. It also carried life-support systems—equipment that helps humans survive in space. Zvezda's deliveries made it possible for three people to live and work on the ISS.

The first crew (two Russians and an American) was called Expedition 1. They arrived at the ISS on November 2, 2000, aboard a Russian Soyuz spacecraft. Since that day, the ISS has always had a human crew.

Expedition 1 crew members spent most of their time setting up the ISS and observing Earth until the next module arrived. On February 7, 2001, NASA launched space shuttle *Atlantis* to the ISS. Its mission was to attach the U.S. laboratory Destiny to Unity.

As soon as Destiny was attached, the ISS crew began scientific work. Ever since, Destiny has been a busy place for testing new technologies, making observations, and conducting experiments.

The crew of Expedition 2 (two Americans and a Russian) arrived at the ISS on March 10, 2001, aboard space shuttle *Discovery*. The two crews worked together until March 18. Then the Expedition 1 crew boarded *Discovery* for the return trip to Earth. Expedition 2 stayed on the ISS until August 2001.

U.S. astronaut Susan J. Helms, an Expedition 2 flight engineer, looks out at Earth from a window on Destiny.

THE NATIONS of the ISS

As of 2010, twenty-six nations have taken part in the ISS. They include Canada, Japan, Russia, the United States, and ESA members. ESA members are Austria, Belgium, the Czech Republic, Denmark, Finland, France, Germany, Greece, Ireland, Italy, Luxembourg, the Netherlands, Norway, Portugal, Spain, Sweden, Switzerland, and the United Kingdom. Estonia, Hungary, Poland, and Romania have also worked on the ISS. They are not ESA members, but they work with the ESA.

U.S. and Russian spacecraft have visited the ISS regularly since 2001. Some have been robot spacecraft delivering supplies. Others have carried new crew members. Still others carried new ISS modules and astronauts who were trained to attach them.

Module by module, the ISS grew. It is built around a long structure called a truss. The truss measures 356 feet (109 m) end to end. By the middle of 2010, all but two of the ISS's planned sixteen modules were in place along the truss. At that point, the space station weighed more than 380 tons (344 metric tons, or 344,000 kg).

Inside, the ISS has 29,500 cubic feet (835 cu. m) of space. That's enough for a permanent crew of six to live and work. The ISS has five bedrooms. That's all the sleeping room it will ever need. But the ISS's working space will continue to grow until the last module is attached around December 2011. At that point, it will weigh about 440 tons (400 metric tons) and have about 35,000 cubic feet (1,000 cu. m) of living, working, and storage space.

ISS PHASE 1, ZVEZDA TO PIRS

The ISS was built in three phases. The first module added after Destiny was the main ISS airlock called Quest. An airlock is a chamber where spacewalking astronauts change into and out of their space suits. It has one hatch (tightly locking door) that connects to the inside of the ISS and another hatch that connects to space. It was delivered by space shuttle *Atlantis* in July 2001. It holds space suits for both U.S. astronauts and Russian cosmonauts.

Two months later, a Russian spacecraft delivered Pirs (pier). Pirs is a docking compartment. It gave Russian spacecraft more places to dock with the ISS. It also gave cosmonauts another airlock for their spacewalks. That completed the first phase of building the ISS.

ISS PHASE 2, HARMONY TO POISK

On February 1, 2003, NASA's space program and the ISS suffered a serious setback. Space shuttle *Columbia* broke apart as it reentered Earth's atmosphere. Its entire crew of seven was killed. NASA stopped the shuttle program until it could make changes.

That delayed Phase 2 of ISS construction until October 2007. The first new module was another connecting node called Harmony. Harmony serves as the hub of the ISS for communications, computer operations, and electrical power.

Harmony also gave the ESA a place to attach its laboratory module Columbus. Columbus arrived in February 2008. Besides adding new laboratory stations inside the ISS, it also added four platforms outside for experiments to be done in space.

Also attached to Harmony is the Japanese laboratory Kibo (hope). It took three space shuttle missions between March and July 2008 to install. Kibo is the largest piece of the ISS.

In November 2009, the Russians delivered Poisk (search). Like Pirs, it added a dock for Russian spacecraft, an airlock, and a place to connect laboratories.

ISS PHASE 3, TRANQUILITY TO NAUKA

The final phase of ISS began in February 2010 when space shuttle *Endeavour* delivered a third node called Tranquility. It also carried a dome-shaped observation deck called the Cupola, built by the Italian Space Agency.

THE -*nauts*

Different countries use different terms for space travelers. The terms come from root words in Latin (*astro-* for "star" or *cosmo-* for "universe") or in a country's modern or historic language. We have had American astronauts, Russian cosmonauts, and Chinese taikonauts (from *taikong* for "space" or "cosmos"). When India launches its first human mission, its crew will be vyomanauts (from *vyoma*, Sanskrit for "sky or space").

In May 2010, space shuttle *Atlantis* attached a small Russian laboratory module called Rassvet (dawn) to Zarya. That was probably *Atlantis*'s final mission.

Space shuttle *Discovery*'s final mission is scheduled for September 2010. Its crew will attach Italian-built storage module Leonardo to Unity. *Endeavour* is scheduled for the last space shuttle mission ever when it delivers some equipment to the ISS in March 2011.

ISS construction will end about December 2011. A Russian spacecraft will deliver Nauka (science) to replace Pirs. It will also add more lab space, a rest area, and a backup system to keep the station pointed in the right direction. Pirs will be sent into Earth's atmosphere, where it will burn up.

European Space Agency astronaut Christer Fuglesang does maintenance on the ISS during a space walk in September 2009.

THE FUTURE OF THE ISS

Once it is complete, the ISS will have many more years of life. Its laboratories will continue to develop new knowledge. We will learn much more about how humans and other living things survive and change in orbit. We may discover new materials that can only be made in space. We will see Earth's weather patterns in new ways.

And if we learn the lessons of the ISS well, it will carry us into the future. Around the year 2020, the last astronauts and cosmonauts will leave the ISS behind. But they will be able to celebrate what so many nations accomplished together. And they will be able to plan the world's next great leap into space.

3 DOWN-TO-EARTH *Satellites*

This satellite was launched by the European Space Agency and orbits above Earth. It is part of the Soil Moisture and Ocean Salinity mission, which keeps track of soil moisture on Earth and salt levels in the ocean.

*T*HE GREAT OBSERVATORIES HAVE CHANGED WHAT WE KNOW ABOUT HOW OUR SMALL PLANET FITS INTO A VAST UNIVERSE. AND THE INTERNATIONAL SPACE STATION HAS CHANGED THE WAY WE VIEW OUR FUTURE. WE CAN LIVE IN SPACE AND MAY SOMEDAY BECOME PERMANENT SETTLERS OF OTHER WORLDS.

Those wonders of space technology appeal to our sense of adventure. But the main reasons to launch artificial satellites have always been much more down to earth. Communications satellites make it possible to share information, in an instant, with people around the world. Global Positioning System (GPS) satellites guide travelers. Military spy satellites make it harder for countries to develop dangerous weapons in secret.

All of those satellite systems make people's lives better. But perhaps the most important use of artificial satellites is studying and predicting Earth's weather and climate.

People rely on GPS satellite technology to navigate in cars (above), *boats, and while hiking.*

PREDICTING THE WEATHER

Most people know a lot about the climate where they live. They know what kind of weather to expect in each season of the year. But climate doesn't tell people what the weather will be like on a particular day. In every season, the weather changes from day to day. Some days, conditions can be extreme.

Dangerous storms sometimes seem to strike without warning. But meteorologists (weather scientists) know that isn't true. Storms always have warning signs. We just need the right tools in the right places to see them. Sometimes the best place is high above Earth in a weather satellite.

This meteorologist examines data from a weather satellite.

SAVING *Lives*

On September 8, 1900, a powerful hurricane roared into Galveston, Texas, from the Gulf of Mexico. It struck without warning, damaging thousands of homes and businesses and killing about eight thousand people.

One day and 108 years later, on September 9, 2008, Hurricane Ike struck Galveston with similar force. This time people were prepared. Weather satellites had tracked Ike across the Atlantic Ocean. Meteorologists issued warnings before it hit land. Most people in its track escaped to safety.

Ike caused billions of dollars in property damage. But this time, two hundred people died. Weather satellite technology saved thousands of lives in that storm alone.

Warning people about dangerous weather is important. But people and businesses also use weather forecasts to help them plan ahead. Farmers use forecasts to decide when to plant or harvest their fields or orchards. Airlines use forecasts to choose the best and safest routes for airplanes. People use forecasts to know what clothes to wear or to plan activities.

One important technology for weather forecasting is computing. Meteorologists have powerful computers. Those computers run programs called weather or climate models. The programs compute what the weather map will look like hours, days, and even weeks ahead.

To predict the weather, models start with the most up-to-date weather measurements available. They produce weather maps with lots of detail. But their forecasts are only as good as the weather measurements that go into them.

That's where this chapter's wonder of space technology comes in. Thanks to weather satellites, meteorologists can add more and better measurements to their climate models.

WEATHER EYES IN THE SKY

Weather is the movement of air and water in the atmosphere. The movement can be in any direction—east, west, north, south, up, or down. Heat, pressure, and Earth's rotation cause the movements.

Sometimes the movements create large differences in temperature or pressure over short distances. For example, a mass of warm air may run into a mass of cool air. The result is powerful storms. But storms are always part of a much larger weather system. That means good weather forecasting needs both "the big picture" and lots of detailed measurements.

Weather satellites carry two kinds of instruments: imagers and sounders. Imagers produce pictures of weather systems. They show how clouds are forming and moving. Some also show temperature patterns. Their measurements cover a large range from east to west and north to south.

Sounders produce measurements of air temperature, moisture content, and other weather conditions at different altitudes (heights). Storms can gain strength when there are large differences in temperature between the cloud tops and the land or sea surface far below. But sometimes, strong high-altitude winds break up storms. And at very high altitudes, fast-moving air currents called jet streams guide the movement of large weather systems. That is why meteorologists need sounders to measure weather conditions from cloud tops down to the surface and everywhere in between.

Some weather conditions, such as hurricanes, change quickly. For those, meteorologists want a satellite taking pictures and soundings all the time. The satellites of the Geostationary Operational Environmental Satellite (GOES) program do just that. The U.S. National Oceanic and Atmospheric Administration (NOAA) has been launching GOES satellites since 1975.

GOES satellites orbit high above Earth's equator (the imaginary line around Earth halfway between the poles). Their altitude is so great (22,300 miles, or 35,900 km) that it takes twenty-four hours to complete one loop. That means they match Earth's rotation. So, from the ground, a GOES satellite appears stationary. It always looks like it is in the same place in the sky.

GOES satellites give meteorologists the big weather picture. They produce images of about one-third of Earth's surface. Two GOES satellites, together with geostationary satellites launched by the European and Japanese space agencies, give around-the-clock images of the whole world's weather.

NOAA and other agencies also need weather details. So they launch other weather satellites in lower orbits to get a closer look. NOAA's are called Advanced Television Infrared Observation Satellites (TIROS-N, or ATN).

The first TIROS satellite went into orbit in 1960. NOAA began developing TIROS-N about ten years later. NOAA keeps two TIROS-N satellites in special orbits at 515 and 540 miles (830 and

This photo shows a rocket taking off carrying a GOES satellite.

"Satellites are vital in predicting where and when tropical storms, hurricanes, floods, cyclones, forest fires . . . may strike."

—*University of Georgia professor and former NASA meteorologist J. Marshall Shepherd, 2002*

870 km) above Earth. They orbit almost (but not quite) over the North Pole and the South Pole. The satellites collect images and other data and send them back to meteorologists on Earth.

These orbits are carefully selected. When the satellites cross the equator on the daylight side of Earth, it is always the same time of day at the point of Earth's surface directly below them. (One satellite crosses the equator in the morning, and one crosses in the afternoon.) That means that the sunlight is always coming from exactly the same angle. That makes it easy to compare pictures of the same area taken on different days.

The satellites complete forty orbits in three days, or one orbit every 108 minutes. So they produce a set of images of forty different regions on Earth. Then they repeat the same set of images with the same lighting three days later.

How Good Are Weather Forecasts?

Thanks to GOES, TIROS, and the weather satellites of other nations, meteorologists have excellent tools for predicting the weather. You have probably seen the results. Weather forecasts on television or on the Internet usually include images from satellites. Broadcasts and Web pages also often use weather models to predict changing conditions hour by hour.

Those forecasts continue to get better as each new weather satellite carries more advanced technology into orbit. Whether people need to prepare for a dangerous storm or plan a picnic, weather satellites are making life safer, better, and more predictable every day.

4 Moon Bases AND MOON WATER

Earth and the Moon as seen from space. Many people think it is only a matter of time before humans live on the Moon.

*I*T'S HARD TO PREDICT WHERE SPACE TECHNOLOGY WILL TAKE US IN THE FUTURE. BUT THE NEXT STEP IN HUMAN SPACE EXPLORATION WILL PROBABLY BE A PERMANENT HUMAN BASE ON THE MOON. LIKE THE INTERNATIONAL SPACE STATION, THIS PROJECT WILL PROBABLY INVOLVE MANY COUNTRIES.

The equipment and the supplies to get the base started will be delivered from Earth. But eventually, the base will need to use the Moon's own resources. And no resource will be more important than water.

U.S. astronaut Edwin "Buzz" Aldrin became the first human to walk on the Moon in 1969.

HOW MOON BASES WILL USE WATER

As they do on Earth, humans on the Moon will need water to live. The Apollo astronauts carried water with them aboard their spacecraft. Will Moon-base astronauts use water from Earth as the Apollo astronauts did? No. The problem is cost.

It costs about ten thousand dollars to deliver 1 pint (0.5 liters) of water to the Moon. A person drinks about 4 pints (2 liters) of water each day. That's forty thousand dollars for water for each day an astronaut spends on the Moon. And that doesn't count the water astronauts would need to prepare food.

Astronauts on a Moon base would need to recycle as much water as possible, even from urine. (They already recycle that on the ISS.) But the base would still need to replace a lot of water every day. And that water would have to come from the Moon itself.

People also need oxygen to breathe. On the Moon base, just as on the ISS, most of that oxygen will come from water. Water is made up of oxygen and hydrogen atoms. The Moon base will have special equipment that separates the oxygen and hydrogen.

Creating a base where people can eat, drink, breathe, and stay comfortable will be a wonder of space technology. But that great achievement of the future will be possible only because other technological wonders have found water on the Moon.

A LUNAR Greenhouse

Once a lunar base begins to grow, one of its most important buildings will be its greenhouse. Greenhouses are buildings used for growing plants. The lunar greenhouse will do more than just supply fresh food. When people breathe, they release carbon dioxide. That has to be removed from the air, or the air becomes unbreathable. Plants take in carbon dioxide and put out oxygen.

People also produce waste products from normal activities such as cooking or using the toilet. Composting (collecting that waste and allowing it to decay naturally) can produce nutrition for plants. So a greenhouse plus a composting unit can keep a Moon base in balance. Scientists are already testing ideas for a lunar greenhouse and composting unit in Antarctica.

ICE ON THE MOON

For many years, scientists thought that the Moon had no water. The Moon's gravitational pull is not strong enough to hold onto an atmosphere. Without an atmosphere, water can't exist as a liquid. Moon water could exist only as vapor (gas) or as ice.

Any vapor would quickly escape into space. And ice wouldn't last long on the Moon either. As soon as the Sun shone on it, lunar ice would turn to water vapor. So even if a huge chunk of ice (such as a comet) hit the Moon, it would soon evaporate and escape into space.

But in the early 1960s, some scientists realized that the Sun never shines on a few places on the Moon. Its north and south poles never fully face the Sun. There, the daytime Sun is always very low in the sky.

The Sun is so low that sunlight never reaches the bottoms of craters near the poles. The permanent darkness keeps the temperature in those craters at a frigid −280°F (−173°C) or colder. At that temperature, ice never melts or evaporates.

This image shows the Moon's north pole. The dark areas are craters. Sunlight never reaches the bottoms of the craters, so the ice within never melts.

So the question became whether ice could form on the Moon in the first place. Scientists realized that it could. They knew that in the solar system's early history, comets rained down on Earth and the Moon. Comets are mostly ice. On Earth they melted and gave our planet plenty of water. On the Moon, they made craters and left some ice behind. Sunlight turned most of that ice to water vapor, which drifted away into space. But some of the water vapor drifted to the craters near the pole and turned back to ice.

If that idea was correct, the Moon's polar craters could still hold ice. But do they?

THE LONG SEARCH FOR LUNAR WATER

It took forty years of space missions to answer that question. But it was worth the wait.

The search for water on the Moon began with the Apollo program. Apollo astronauts visited the Moon between 1969 and 1972. One of their major tasks was to collect rocks. The minerals in those rocks told scientists a lot about the Moon's history.

The Apollo astronauts did not visit the Moon's polar regions. So NASA scientists couldn't use Moon rocks to test the idea of polar ice. Finally, in 1994, a spacecraft named *Clementine* used radar to look into some of those permanently shadowed polar craters. The radar signals showed the crater floors were much smoother than the rest of the Moon.

One explanation for that smoothness was ice. But *Clementine* had no instruments to look for water.

The next mission to look for ice was the Lunar *Prospector* in 1998. The *Prospector* spacecraft spent a year orbiting the Moon at its polar regions. It carried an instrument to look for hydrogen atoms. Hydrogen would be a good sign that there's water. *Prospector* found lots of hydrogen in the bottoms of the polar craters.

"Every place on the Moon, at some point during the lunar day . . . has water."

—Jessica Sunshine, senior research scientist, University of Maryland, 2009

That probably meant there was water, but scientists wanted to be sure. So in July 1999, at the end of its mission, *Prospector* fired its control rockets one last time. It crashed into Shoemaker Crater near the Moon's south pole and sent up a plume of matter.

Scientists on Earth watched that plume carefully. But their telescopes did not pick up any water in that plume. Neither did the *Cassini-Huygens* spacecraft as it passed by the Moon on the way to Saturn. That was puzzling. Ice was still the best explanation for the hydrogen. So scientists looked for reasonable explanations for not seeing any water. Perhaps *Prospector* crashed in a spot where there was very little ice. Still, if they were hoping for a definite answer, they were disappointed.

This drawing of the Lunar Prospector *shows the spacecraft in orbit. The three arms extending from the craft are called masts, or booms. They contain* Prospector's *instruments.*

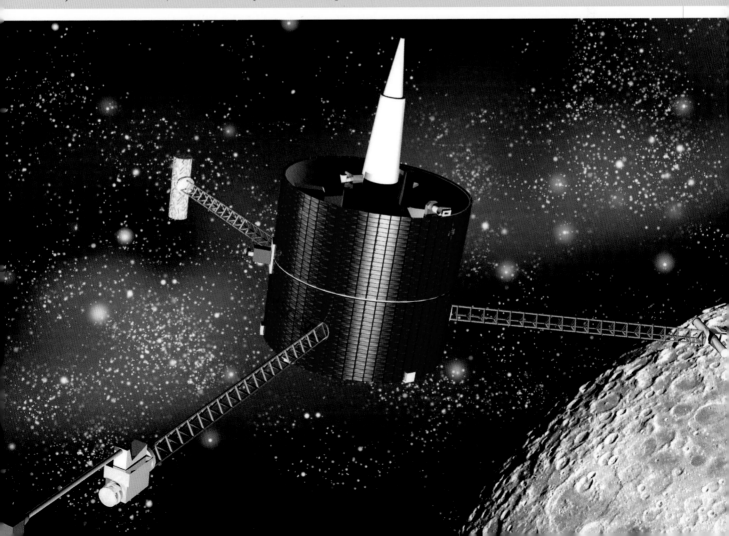

The first detection of real lunar water came in 2008. Apollo astronauts had brought back some lunar soil that contained tiny volcanic beads. Researchers studying the beads found very slight traces of water trapped inside them. But the soil was still far drier than any desert on Earth. If the soil ever held any other water, it had evaporated and drifted into space.

Finally, in 2009, two different missions to the Moon produced that long-sought definite answer—and a big surprise. Not only was there ice in those polar craters, but there was also usable water almost everywhere on the Moon.

That surprise came from *Chandrayaan-1*. That was the first mission to the Moon by the Indian Space Research Organisation (ISRO). *Chandrayaan-1* was launched on October 22, 2008. It carried two NASA instruments, including the Moon Mineralogy Mapper (M^3).

M^3 maps where different minerals can be found on the Moon. It creates images of the Moon in infrared light. Infrared light has a wide range of wavelengths. Each substance, such as rock or water, reflects or absorbs certain infrared wavelengths. That means each substance has a distinctive infrared "color." And that's how M^3 produced its maps.

On September 24, 2009, NASA and ISRO announced that M^3 detected water on the Moon. The water signal was strongest at the poles, where it was expected. But there was also water everywhere else.

Where did that water come from? Scientists realized that another long-held idea about water on the Moon also made sense. The Sun sends out more than

This image was taken by the Moon Mineralogy Mapper. It shows the different materials found on the side of the Moon that faces Earth.

*"The Moon has put out a welcome mat.
What are we waiting for?"*
—Paul D. Spudis, senior staff scientist, Lunar and Planetary Institute,
Houston, Texas, 2009

light. It also sends a stream of particles called the solar wind. Most of those particles are electrically charged hydrogen atoms. Many of the Moon's minerals contain oxygen. The hydrogen from the solar wind combines with that oxygen to form water.

During the lunar day, water molecules form faster than they evaporate into space. So the Moon is always slightly damp. The water evaporates quickly when the Sun sets and the solar wind ends, but more water forms again the next day. Scientists think that enough water forms on the Moon's surface to support a human settlement. That means that a base would not have to be set up near the icy polar craters. It could probably be set up almost anywhere on the Moon.

M^3's discovery was a cause for great celebration among space travel fans. But it wasn't their only reason to cheer. The NASA Lunar Crater Observation and Sensing Satellite (LCROSS) was coming to the spectacular end of its mission.

NASA had launched LCROSS on June 18, 2009. As LCROSS neared the Moon, the craft's rocket booster fired. It put itself and LCROSS into a long looping Earth orbit. On October 9, the booster fired again, sending itself and LCROSS toward the Moon's south pole. NASA scientists wanted the craft to crash into the polar Cabeus Crater.

After separating from LCROSS, the booster fired its engines for the final time. It was now traveling just ahead of LCROSS. It crashed into Cabeus, sending up a plume of debris. Four minutes later, LCROSS flew through the plume and sent back measurements about what was in it. Then LCROSS crashed. It created a second plume for observers on Earth and satellites orbiting the Moon to study.

The plumes were not as spectacular as the observers on Earth hoped for. But the results of both impacts were clear. Unlike the *Prospector* crash, this time there was no doubt. Cabeus Crater was full of ice!

Thanks to those discoveries by *Chandrayaan-1* and LCROSS, the next great wonder of space technology may be a permanent human base on the Moon.

5 MARS Rovers

This NASA artist's image shows the rover Spirit on Mars. The rover was launched in 2003.

$\mathcal{T}$O MANY SCIENTISTS, NO IDEA IS MORE EXCITING THAN THE THOUGHT OF EXPLORING MARS. THEY PROBABLY WON'T BE ABLE TO GO IN PERSON UNTIL THE 2040S, BUT THEY HAVE FOUND ANOTHER WAY. SCIENTISTS EXPLORE THE RED PLANET THROUGH SOME OF THE GREATEST WONDERS OF SPACE TECHNOLOGY EVER BUILT. FROM THEIR LABORATORIES ON EARTH, THEY CONTROL ROBOT ROVERS ON THE MARTIAN SURFACE.

Mars is known as the Red Planet. It is often easily visible from Earth.

Looking for Life on Mars

Mars has fascinated scientists for a long time. In the late nineteenth century, astronomer Percival Lowell built an observatory in Flagstaff, Arizona. Lowell used his telescope to observe Mars as often as he could.

In 1894 Lowell knew that Mars was closer to Earth than it would be again for several years. Mars was high in the sky at midnight and visible from Earth all night long. Lowell used this chance to closely observe the planet. Telescopic photography was not very advanced at that time. So Lowell drew what he saw through the telescope—a map of Mars crisscrossed with straight lines.

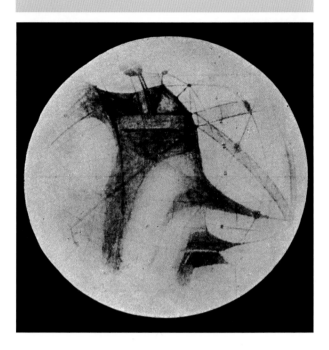

This 1896 drawing by Percival Lowell shows the "canals" that Lowell thought crossed the surface of Mars.

To Lowell, the lines were evidence that Mars was home to intelligent life. He thought they were canals, or artificial waterways. He believed they were built by creatures that could think and plan. He thought those canals carried water from the polar caps to farms and towns that needed it badly.

But Lowell's map and his conclusions were wrong. In the 1960s, spacecraft took the first close-up pictures of Mars. The pictures showed that Mars's surface was full of craters. Most of the craters were too small to be seen by Lowell's telescope. At best, they would have looked like dots. Human brains naturally connect dots into lines. Lowell's brain fooled him into seeing canals.

Lowell was wrong about intelligent Martians. But the idea of life on other worlds continues to drive people to learn more about Mars and its history. Even if Mars never had intelligent life, perhaps it had simpler life-forms, such as bacteria. Perhaps simple life-forms still live on Mars.

The best way to find out is to land a spacecraft on Mars. And the best kind of craft is one that can move over the surface of the planet on its own. That is why scientists designed, built, and sent robot rovers to Mars.

How Rovers Are Named

Each time a rover mission to Mars is planned, NASA holds a contest for students. Students are invited to write an essay suggesting a name for the latest robot explorer. For the Pathfinder mission, NASA asked students to suggest a heroine. The winning choice was Sojourner Truth, an African American woman who lived in the 1800s. Truth was a former slave who wrote about human rights. Later contests allowed students to suggest nonhuman names. The winning choices reflected the adventure of exploration—**Spirit**, **Opportunity**, and **Curiosity**.

SOJOURNER

The first rover to land on Mars was NASA's *Sojourner*. It was about the size of a microwave oven and weighed about 23 pounds (10.5 kg). *Sojourner* arrived on July 4, 1997, as part of a larger spacecraft called *Mars Pathfinder*.

Pathfinder used a new technology for landing on another planet. Parachutes carried *Pathfinder* to within 1 mile (1.6 km) of the surface of Mars. Then descent rockets fired to slow it down. As the spacecraft neared the surface, air bags inflated around it. Finally, *Pathfinder* was released from the parachutes. It must have looked like a large ball of Bubble

Mars Pathfinder *was launched on December 4, 1996, aboard a rocket* (left). Pathfinder *carried the* Sojourner *rover to Mars.*

In this image, Sojourner *sits on one of* Pathfinder's *ramps, waiting to roll onto the surface of Mars. The photo was taken by a* Pathfinder *camera on July 4, 1997.*

Wrap as it hit the ground at 23 miles (37 km) per hour. It bounced at least three times and then rolled to its resting place.

Besides cushioning the impact, the air bags also prevented *Pathfinder* from getting stuck on a rock. Once it came to rest, the air bags deflated, and *Pathfinder* opened up like petals on a flower. Those petals served as ramps for *Sojourner* to roll down to the Martian surface.

Pathfinder's cameras immediately started scanning its surroundings. It sent photos back to thrilled scientists on Earth. Once they saw where the spacecraft had landed, they began planning *Sojourner's* exploration. While *Sojourner* roamed, *Pathfinder* would stay in one place as a stationary base.

Scientists expected *Sojourner* to work for only a week to a month. But it rolled across the surface on its six wheels for almost three months—until September 27, 1997. Its top speed was a snail-like 0.4 inches (1 centimeter) per second. But the rover lasted long enough to explore about 0.3 miles (500 m) from *Pathfinder* in many directions.

Sojourner examined rocks and soil up close in sixteen locations. Scientists named some of the rocks after cartoon characters, such as Barnacle Bill, Scooby-Doo, and Yogi. Meanwhile, *Pathfinder* sent 8.5 million measurements of weather conditions and more than 16,500 photographs to scientists.

"Spirit is not dead; it has just entered another phase of its long life."
—Doug McCuiston, director of NASA's Mars Exploration Program, 2010

SPIRIT AND OPPORTUNITY

The next major rover mission involved twin rovers, *Spirit* and *Opportunity*. *Spirit* launched first, on June 10, 2003. *Opportunity* followed on July 7. On January 4 and 27, 2004, they landed on opposite sides of Mars for three-month missions.

Unlike *Sojourner*, *Spirit* and *Opportunity* did not have a stationary base. They each weighed about 400 pounds (185 kg). They measured 4.9 feet (1.5 m) high, 7.5 feet (2.3 m) wide, and 5.2 feet (1.6 m) long. Each rover sat on a six-wheeled frame that could carry it over small rocks if necessary. The rovers were built for a top speed of about 2 inches (5 cm) per second, but they rarely went that fast.

NASA scientists soon realized that the sturdy rovers could keep going well beyond their planned three months. The agency extended the mission many times. Day after day, the rovers rolled into and out of craters. They studied rocks up close and explored many types of terrain. They sent back data and images that showed signs that Mars once had flowing water and lakes or seas.

Opportunity continues to roll. But *Spirit*'s travels ended on May 6, 2009, after about 4.8 miles (7.7 km). One of its wheels got stuck in crusty soil. Two other wheels had already broken, and the mission scientists could not get *Spirit* unstuck.

Still, scientists could learn plenty about the sand around *Spirit*'s wheel and about the nearby rocks and stones. So they kept taking

This image of Opportunity *rolling across the surface of Mars was made by combining NASA photos of the rover and the Mars surface.*

measurements and looking for new ways to free *Spirit*.

On January 26, 2010, scientists had to change plans. Winter was coming to *Spirit*'s region of Mars. So scientists prepared the rover for "hibernation." During hibernation, *Spirit* stops most activities. It uses just enough energy to keep its equipment warm and its batteries charged during the six-month Martian winter. (Mars's seasons are about twice as long as Earth's.)

Scientists took measurements as long as *Spirit*'s solar cells could generate enough energy. That ended on March 30, 2010, when *Spirit* went into full hibernation.

They then planned a new mission. Starting in the Martian spring, *Spirit*'s new task is to measure tiny wobbles in Mars's rotation. That will tell scientists whether Mars's core is solid or liquid. The measurements can only be done if the rover stays in one place.

They didn't know for certain that *Spirit* would survive the winter. But they knew not to give up on a robot that had already operated twenty-four times as long as expected. In fact, *Spirit* managed to move about a foot (0.3 m) before finally entering hibernation. If it restarts in the spring and manages to climb out of its trap, it may go back to roving after all.

A ROVER NAMED *CURIOSITY*

If all goes according to schedule, the next Mars rover will blast off in September 2011. It will land on Mars in mid-2012. Its official name will be the Mars Science Laboratory (MSL). But thanks to a grade-school student from Kansas named Clara Ma, most people will call it *Curiosity*.

The MSL will be a technological wonder even before it sends its first signals from the Martian surface. Just reaching the ground will require a very clever piece of engineering called a sky crane.

The MSL will weigh about 1 ton (0.9 metric tons), not counting the sky crane and the protective shell that will get it safely through the Martian atmosphere. The MSL is about the size of a small car. Given its weight and size, it will need more than air bags to land safely. As it enters Mars's atmosphere, parachutes will begin to slow its descent.

After the parachutes have slowed the MSL down, the shell holding the sky crane and the rover will open up. A sky crane platform will begin its descent,

This 2009 NASA drawing shows what Curiosity will look like on the surface of Mars.

with the rover dangling below it on cables. Small rockets will fire to slow the platform until it is hovering not far above the surface. When the rover's wheels touch the Martian surface, tools powered by explosives will cut the cables.

After *Curiosity* lands, it will be ready to start its planned exploration. It will be able to roll over rocks as tall as 30 inches (75 cm). Its top speed will be 1 inch (2.5 cm) per second. That's half of *Spirit*'s and *Opportunity*'s top speed. But *Curiosity*'s average pace is expected to be faster. It is expected to cover 12 miles (19 km) in one Mars year (686 Earth days). It took *Opportunity* more than three times as long to travel that far.

Curiosity's cameras and tools will almost certainly make important discoveries. What it finds will pave the way for future human missions to Mars. And that first Mars year might only be the beginning of a much longer mission for the rover.

It is fun to imagine what might happen if *Curiosity* outlasts its planned mission length by as much as *Spirit* and *Opportunity* did. If that happens, it might still be sending back data to Earth when the first humans arrive to check out the Red Planet for themselves.

"Curiosity is the passion that drives us through our everyday lives. We have become explorers and scientists with our need to ask questions and to wonder."

—*Kansas student Clara Ma, in her winning 2009 essay to name a Mars rover*

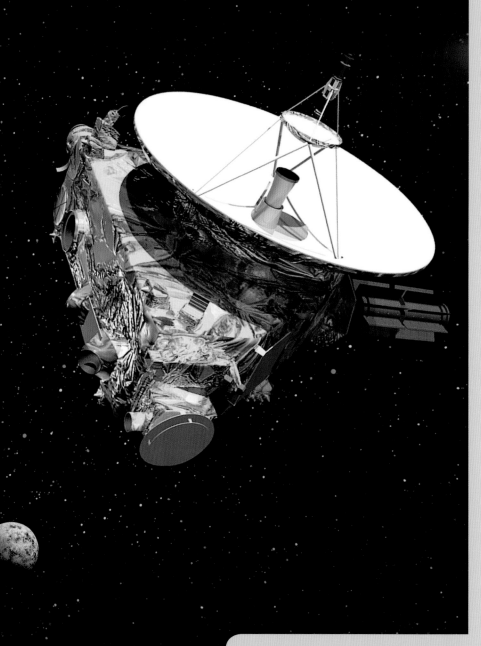

6 New Horizons

New Horizons *approaches Pluto and its three known moons in this artist's image.* New Horizons *will reach Pluto in 2015.*

$\mathcal{W}$HAT COULD STRETCH THE HORIZONS OF HUMAN KNOWLEDGE MORE THAN A VISIT TO THE VAST OUTER REACHES OF THE SOLAR SYSTEM? THAT IS WHY NASA CHOSE THE NAME NEW HORIZONS FOR ITS MISSION TO EXPLORE THE PART OF THE SOLAR SYSTEM KNOWN AS THE KUIPER BELT.

The Kuiper Belt is a region beyond the planet Neptune. It includes many large icy bodies called Kuiper Belt Objects (KBOs). The most famous KBO is the dwarf planet Pluto.

The region is named for Dutch-born American astronomer Gerard Kuiper. Kuiper was one of the twentieth century's greatest astronomers. In 1951 Kuiper described his ideas about how the solar system formed. Kuiper said that when the solar system was young, lots of smaller bodies orbited in that distant region. He thought that Pluto formed when many of those small KBOs came together.

At that time, scientists thought that Pluto was about as large as Earth. If so, Pluto's gravity would have been strong enough to change the orbits of the remaining KBOs. They would leave the region, either moving inward toward the Sun or outward. That would leave Pluto as the only body left orbiting in that part of the solar system.

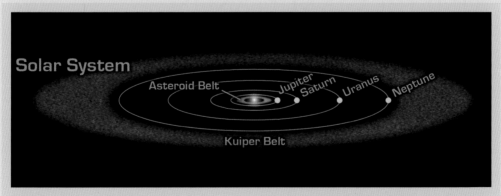

This diagram of the solar system shows the planets and the Kuiper Belt.

Pluto (right) *orbits in the Kuiper Belt at an average distance of 3.7 billion miles (6 billion km) from the Sun.*

Astronomers thought that Kuiper was probably right about the early Kuiper Belt. But as they learned more about Pluto, they realized that it is only 18 percent as large as Earth and 1/500th as heavy. It was too small to be the only KBO. Its gravity is too weak to change the orbits of the other KBOs very much. So astronomers started using their telescopes to look for other KBOs besides Pluto.

In 1992 they found the first one. By 2002 they had found more than one hundred. They also realized that KBOs had much more to teach than what could be seen through telescopes. It was time to work on a spacecraft that could travel far enough to visit Pluto and the Kuiper Belt.

BEYOND THE GIANT PLANETS

Before *New Horizons,* only one other spacecraft had ever visited worlds beyond the orbit of Saturn. That craft, NASA's *Voyager 2,* was launched on August 20, 1977. (Its twin, *Voyager 1,* launched on September 5, 1977.) At that time, the Sun's giant planets—Jupiter, Saturn, Uranus, and Neptune—were lined up so *Voyager 2* could explore all four. It passed close to Jupiter in 1979, Saturn in 1981, Uranus in 1986, and Neptune in 1989.

Pluto was in the wrong part of its orbit for *Voyager 2* to reach it. So visiting the last of the nine major planets (as Pluto was still considered then) would have to wait.

In 1989 scientists thought the cost of sending a probe just to visit cold, distant Pluto was too high. The mission just wouldn't produce enough scientific knowledge for the price. But once astronomers realized how much there was to learn about the Kuiper Belt, they were eager to explore Pluto and other KBOs. They wanted to test the ideas of many astronomers (including Kuiper) about the early history of the solar system.

They started planning the New Horizons mission. On January 19, 2006, a NASA rocket sent the spacecraft on its way to the Kuiper Belt. When it reaches that icy region, the first bodies to explore will be Pluto and its moons—especially the largest one, Charon.

Only a few months after *New Horizons* launched, an international group of astronomers met. They decided that Pluto should no longer be considered a major planet. One reason for that decision was the discovery of another KBO larger than Pluto. That KBO—Eris—was discovered in 2003 and measured in 2005. The astronomers decided to put Pluto, Eris, and Ceres (the largest asteroid in the solar system) in a different category. They were classified as dwarf planets.

Some astronomers and many other people were disappointed that Pluto was no longer counted as a major planet. But the decision didn't matter to the New Horizons scientists. Whether it is a planet or a KBO, Pluto—and the entire Kuiper Belt—is important to planetary astronomy.

NEW HORIZONS'S PATH TO PLUTO

When the *New Horizons* spacecraft reaches Pluto, it will be about one-third farther from the Sun than Neptune. Traveling that far will take a long time. But NASA did two things to make it faster.

First, NASA put *New Horizons* on top of a rocket booster that sent it into space faster than any other space probe in history. It left Earth at a record-breaking speed of 10 miles (16 km) per second. That compares to about 7 miles (11 km) per second for past missions to the Moon or Mars.

Once the rocket shut off, Earth's gravity slowed it down a little. But in only nine hours, *New Horizons* was farther from Earth than the Moon is. Soon it was so far away from Earth that its path was controlled by the Sun's gravity.

New Horizons was then in a long oval path around the Sun, more like a comet's orbit than a planet's. Its speed was about 100,000 miles (162,000 km) per hour.

The farther it got from the Sun, the slower *New Horizons* traveled. Still, it crossed Mars's orbit on April 6, 2006, only seventy-seven days after launch. It approached Jupiter's orbit in late February 2007. By then it had slowed to about 43,000 miles (70,000 km) per hour.

The craft was on a course that would carry it to Pluto in 2018. That was when mission planners used their second trip-shortening idea. They got a boost from Jupiter's gravity—called a gravity assist.

As *New Horizons* crossed Jupiter's orbit, the giant planet was not far away. On February 28, the spacecraft came within 1.4 million miles (2.3 million km) of Jupiter. The tug of the planet's powerful gravity made *New Horizons* speed up and change direction. After it left Jupiter's influence, it was moving at about 52,000 miles (84,000 km) per hour. It was on a new orbit that would carry it close to Pluto in July 2015.

A MATTER
of Speed

How fast was *New Horizons* traveling when it first went into its orbit around the Sun? There are 3,600 seconds in an hour. That means the *New Horizons* speed of 100,000 miles (160,000 km) per hour works out to about 28 miles (45 km) per second. But *New Horizons* started out moving away from Earth at 10 miles (16 km) per second and slowed down. So how is 28 miles per second possible? The answer is that Earth is moving around the Sun at 18.6 miles (30 km) per second. You have to add the two motions—of *New Horizons* and of Earth—together to get the speed of the spacecraft around the Sun.

The New Horizons *spacecraft takes off from the launchpad aboard a rocket in January 2006.*

Doing a Lot with a Little

Spacecraft designers can't do everything they want to do. They can't include all the features they'd like. And they don't have unlimited money to develop all the new technology they'd like. So they design their missions to make the most of the technology they have. They learn to do a lot with a little.

Each instrument a spacecraft carries adds weight. The heavier a craft is, the more energy it needs to launch into space. The designers of *New Horizons* knew that they needed to launch at high speed. More weight and more speed both call for more fuel and a bigger rocket. They put their scientific wishlist together with their technology and came to a decision.

The final design included the *New Horizons* spacecraft and all its instruments, communications equipment, and a small rocket engine to adjust its course. It was about the size of a grand piano and weighed 1,054 pounds (478 kg). Of that, only 66 pounds (30 kg) was scientific instruments. But NASA calls that collection of seven measurement tools "the most capable . . . ever launched on a first . . . mission to an unexplored planet."

The Kuiper Belt region gets only 1/1600th the amount of sunlight Earth gets. So *New Horizons*'s instruments were designed to work in extreme cold and darkness. Even more remarkable is that all the instruments put together only need 28 watts of electric power. That's only 70 percent of what a typical refrigerator lightbulb needs!

Let's look at each of the instruments, starting with Alice. This 9.9-pound (4.5 kg) device will study the atmosphere of Pluto and its largest moon Charon using ultraviolet light. The UV light will tell Alice how much of what gases are in those atmospheres. It will also produce pictures that show where those gases are. And it will measure the temperature at different levels of those atmospheres. It will do all that using only 4.4 watts of power.

Astronomers also want to know about the surfaces of KBOs—what they look like, what they are made of, and what their temperatures are. Ralph is a 22.7-pound (10.3 kg) package of cameras. The cameras will use ordinary visible light and infrared light to produce maps and pictures of every KBO that *New Horizons* visits. Ralph uses only 6.3 watts of power.

The Radio Science Experiment (REX) weighs a mere 3.5 ounces (100 grams) and uses 2.1 watts of power. It will receive radio signals beamed from Earth as *New Horizons* passes behind Pluto, Charon, and other KBOs. The amount the radio signals bend as they pass through Pluto's atmosphere will tell scientists about the atmosphere's gases. If Charon and the other KBOs have atmospheres, REX will detect them as well.

As *New Horizons* approaches Pluto, the world will be eager for pictures. The photographer will be the spacecraft's Long Range Reconnaissance Imager (LORRI). At 19.4 pounds (8.8 kg), LORRI is the heaviest of *New Horizons*'s instruments. It will use 5.8 watts of power, almost as much power as Ralph.

In late December 2014 or early January 2015, about two hundred days before *New Horizons* reaches Pluto, LORRI will take its first pictures. Pluto and its moons will be just dots in those images. But their locations will help scientists on Earth steer *New Horizons*. They will send *New Horizons* a command to fire its control rockets so it passes Pluto in the best possible location.

As *New Horizons* gets closer to Pluto, LORRI's close-up images will get sharper and more detailed. At *New Horizons*'s closest approach, it will probably be about 6,000 miles (10,000 km) from Pluto. From that distance, LORRI's photos will show objects as small as a football field. Scientists won't be the only people to be thrilled when LORRI snaps those pictures. They will probably be splashed on the front pages of websites and newspapers all around the world.

A 7.3-pound (3.3 kg) *New Horizons* instrument called SWAP is named for what it is designed to study, the solar wind at Pluto. It requires 2.3 watts of power.

The Sun puts out a stream of high-energy electrically charged particles called the solar wind. Scientists know how those particles interact with Earth's upper atmosphere and magnetic field. They also know that it creates a faint straight tail visible on some comets besides their bright, curved dusty tail.

HOW ALICE AND RALPH *Got Their Names*

The names of some spacecraft instruments mean something important. But most are acronyms. An acronym is a word or name made of the first letters of a phrase, such as REX or LORRI. So do Alice and Ralph mean something scientific? No. Alice and Ralph are the names of two characters from a 1950s TV show, *The Honeymooners*. *New Horizons* lead scientist Alan Stern chose the names.

NASA workers attach the SWAP instrument to the New Horizons *spacecraft. SWAP will allow scientist to study the solar winds at Pluto.*

Pluto has a weak gravity that allows its atmosphere to escape into space. Some scientists suspect that Pluto may lose up to 165 pounds (75 kg) of atmosphere every second. If that's true, Pluto will have a straight trail behind it, making it look like a super-sized comet. By measuring Pluto's interaction with the solar wind, SWAP will tell those scientists whether their idea is right or wrong.

SWAP will have a 3.3-pound (1.5 kg), 2.5-watt partner called PEPSSI (Pluto Energetic Particle Spectrometer Science Investigation). SWAP will measure particles from the solar wind itself. PEPSSI will look for atoms and molecules that have escaped from Pluto's atmosphere. PEPSSI's detector is sensitive enough to pick up a whiff of escaped atmosphere while *New Horizons* is still millions of miles (and several days) away from Pluto.

Because NASA is interested in education as well as research, they held a competition to choose one instrument designed and built by college students. The winning entry came from students at the University of Colorado at Boulder. Their instrument, the 5-watt, 4.2-pound (1.9 kg) Venetia Burney Student Dust Counter (VB-SDC, or simply SDC), began working almost as soon as *New Horizons* left Earth.

VB-SDC's job is to count and measure microscopic dust grains in space. Those tiny particles are produced by collisions among asteroids, comets, and KBOs. Near Pluto, dust may also come from collisions of small objects with Nix, Hydra, or other small moons of Pluto. The farthest that a dust detector ever flew was about 1.7 billion miles (2.8 billion km) from the Sun. VB-SDC will more than double that distance to 3.6 billion miles (5.8 billion km).

WHO WAS *Venetia Burney?*

In June 2006, the SDC was named in honor of Venetia Burney. In 1930 Venetia was an eleven-year-old student in Oxford, England. That year astronomer Clyde Tombaugh discovered a planet (as it was considered then) beyond Neptune. Venetia suggested the name Pluto to her grandfather, Falconer Madan. Madan contacted an astronomer who knew Tombaugh. Tombaugh liked the name Pluto, and it was soon made official. Venetia Burney Phair lived to see *New Horizons* launched. She died in 2009.

OTHER JOBS FOR *NEW HORIZONS*

VB-SDC began counting and measuring dust particles soon after it left Earth. NASA is also using other *New Horizons* instruments along the way to Pluto. On June 13, 2006, *New Horizons* flew within 63,400 miles (102,000 km) of

"Exploring Pluto and the Kuiper Belt is like conducting an archaeological dig into the history of the outer solar system, a place where we can peek into the ancient era of planetary formation."
—*Alan Stern*, New Horizons *lead scientist, 2006*

an asteroid that had been discovered in 2002. Its instruments measured the asteroid's size, color, and shape.

A few months later, *New Horizons* flew by Jupiter. All of its instruments got a workout. Alice and Ralph worked together to study Jupiter's auroras (streams of light near the planet's poles) and its four largest moons.

REX tested its instruments by picking up radio signals produced by Jupiter's atmosphere. LORRI took a lot of photos, especially to study its rings and some small moons. SWAP and PEPSSI made measurements of high-energy charged particles in Jupiter's magnetic field. VB-SDC looked for dust in the same region.

All the *New Horizon* instruments did their job at Jupiter. Next stops: Pluto, Charon, and beyond!

Cameras on New Horizons *took photos of Jupiter and its moon Io as the craft flew by the planet in 2007.*

7 FUTURE TECHNOLOGIES FOR Space Travel

A Soyuz *spacecraft launches in Kazakhstan in 2009. Scientists are constantly working to improve spacecraft technology.*

*A*LL THE SIX OTHER WONDERS OF SPACE
TECHNOLOGY IN THIS BOOK HAVE ONE IMPORTANT INGREDIENT IN
COMMON. THEY COULD NOT HAVE REACHED SPACE WITHOUT A ROCKET.

Compared to everyday transportation, rockets reach amazing speeds. Traveling at its normal speed, a passenger jet would need about two days to go around the world at the equator. The rocket that launched *New Horizons* traveled that distance in forty-five minutes!

But even at that amazing speed, it still took more than a year to reach Jupiter. And even with a gravity assist from Jupiter, it will take nine and half years to reach Pluto.

For some people with big dreams of the future, the rocket that launched *New Horizons* is much too slow. Some of them are dreaming of a human base on Mars with lots of travel between the two planets. They want rockets at least twice as fast as *New Horizons*. Others would like to see human travel to the outer planets. They dream of spacecraft ten times faster than *New Horizons*.

And suppose scientists wanted to send a robot spacecraft to explore another solar system. How fast would that craft have to travel? A spacecraft traveling at the speed of *New Horizons* when it left Earth would take about thirty thousand years to reach the nearest stars to Earth, the Alpha Centauri system. Light from those three stars takes more than four years to reach Earth. Scientists suspect that one of them, Alpha Centauri B, has a solar system with undiscovered planets.

Alpha Centauri (top left) *is a system of three stars. From Earth, without a telescope, the system looks like a single large star.*

Astronomers can study Alpha Centauri from this observatory in Chile in South America. Here the Cerro Tololo Inter-American Observatory (CTIO) is seen at sunset, as it opens its shutters to view the night sky.

What is a reasonable amount of time for scientists to wait for results of a mission to Alpha Centauri B? Thirty-five years? Let's work backward from that number. Once that spacecraft reached its destination, it would take more than four years for its signals to reach Earth. So the craft would have to get to the Alpha Centauri system in a little more than thirty years. That means it would have to travel one thousand times as fast as *New Horizons*!

Are such speedy spacecraft possible? Some scientists think so. They are already working on two new technological wonders for high-speed space travel within our solar system and beyond.

GETTING UP TO SPEED

To understand those new ideas, we need to look first at the rocketry of past and present space missions. All of those have used rocket boosters that work in the same way. Those are called conventional rockets.

Conventional rockets get their power from two chemical substances called the fuel and the oxidizer. When those substances mix, they create a fiery reaction. Together, the fuel and the oxidizer are called propellant.

To launch a craft into space and get it up to speed, conventional rockets burn a lot of propellant in a short time. While the propellant is burning, the rockets produce hot exhaust gases. Those escape at high speed through a nozzle. The exhaust blasts out of the nozzle at a speed of up to 10,000 miles (16,200 km) per hour. The exhaust gases push back on the rocket with a force called thrust. Think of blowing up a balloon and then letting the air out. The collapsing balloon forces the air in one direction. The escaping air produces thrust that sends the balloon flying in the opposite direction.

The amount of thrust depends on how much exhaust the engine creates and how fast the exhaust flows. Rocket engine designers know how to make that exhaust speed as high as possible. That makes the thrust as large as possible.

As long as the propellant is burning, the rocket gains speed. The longer the engine burns, the faster the rocket goes. But there is a limit to the amount of propellant it can carry. The total weight of the rocket, the spacecraft, and the propellant has to be less than the thrust. Otherwise, it will not be able to lift off.

Thanks to conventional rockets, we have been able to send robot spacecraft to explore the entire solar system. We have also used them to send people to the Moon. And we will probably use them for the first human trips to Mars later this century.

But if we want to launch manned spacecraft beyond Mars or unmanned spacecraft to explore other solar systems, conventional rockets will be too slow. So scientists and engineers are developing two new technologies for space travel.

STACKS OF *Rockets*

Rocket boosters for space missions usually use a stack of rockets called stages. The most common number of stages is three. The first stage has the largest thrust because it boosts the most weight. When it runs out of propellant, it falls away. The rocket is then much lighter, so the second stage can produce a greater speed increase with less thrust. When the second stage runs out of propellant, it falls away too. The third stage has the least weight. Its engine gives the spacecraft the final large boost in speed to reach its destination.

One is similar to rocketry. The other is not.

Neither provides as much thrust as conventional rockets. But they both push steadily for a long time. No matter how fast the spacecraft is already traveling, they will be able to make it go faster. Its speed will increase minute by minute, hour after hour, and day after day for a very long time. That will be the secret to reaching the stars! Let's look at each of those new technologies, starting with a centuries-old dream.

SOLAR SAILS

For more than four hundred years, people have been imagining what it would be like to sail through the solar system. In the early seventeenth century, people were sailing the ocean in search of unknown lands. It was natural for astronomers of the age to think about sailing the skies. One of them, Johannes Kepler, wrote, "Let us create vessels and sails adjusted to the heavenly ether [a substance then thought to fill space] and there will be plenty of people unafraid of the empty wastes."

Kepler was right about those fearless explorers. When we created the technology to send people to the Moon, lots of people were ready to take the trip. And others are eager to travel to Mars. But was Kepler also right about sails?

Maybe! The first human missions to Mars will probably use conventional rockets. But in one hundred years, travel to Mars may be very different.

German astronomer Johannes Kepler (1571–1630) wrote about sailing into space in the early seventeenth century. Kepler was also a teacher of mathematics.

PUSHY *Light*

It may be hard to understand how reflecting light can push anything. But imagine you are throwing a "perfect" ball against a wall. A "perfect" ball bounces back without losing any energy of motion. It gives the wall a push, but the wall can't move, so the ball bounces back with as much energy as it came in with. Now replace the wall with a board on rollers. When the ball bounces off the board, it gives the board the same push. But the board can move. So the push transfers some energy from the ball to the board. Light striking a solar sail gives it a push in the same way.

Humans may be living in settlements on Mars. And trips between Earth and Mars may be common. The travelers may be able to shorten their transportation time by sailing on sunlight.

Light is a form of energy. When a light beam hits a mirror, it gives the mirror a push as it bounces off (reflects). If the mirror can't move, the push doesn't transfer any energy. But if the mirror is free to move, the push from the light beam gives the mirror a little bit of its energy. If the mirror reflects a lot of light, those little bits of energy can add up to a lot.

That's the idea behind a solar sail. It is a large, lightweight mirror in space. When sunlight reflects off the sail, it produces a small but constant thrust. That thrust is not enough to lift a spacecraft into orbit. But when a craft is already in space, that steady thrust for days or weeks adds up to a lot of extra speed.

Some space scientists and engineers began testing solar sails in 2005. Their project is called LightSail. LightSail is different from many space technology projects in an important way. Its leadership does not come from a government space agency such as NASA. Instead, LightSail is a project of the Planetary Society (TPS). TPS is an organization of ordinary citizens who are excited about exploring other worlds.

"We have lingered for too long on the shores of the cosmic ocean; it's time to set sail for the stars."
—*Carl Sagan, American astronomer and author, 1980*

The 2005 solar sail test mission failed when the rocket carrying it crashed. TPS hopes to send the next solar sail, LightSail-1, into space sometime in 2011. All they need is to hitch a ride on a rocket with a little extra room.

LightSail-1 is a light, thin sheet of plastic called mylar. The mylar is coated with aluminum. The sail is less than one-tenth as thick as an ordinary sheet of printer paper. It will open up into a square about 18 feet (5.5 m) on each side. Yet it weighs less than 10 pounds (4.5 kg).

The main purpose of LightSail-1 is to practice solar sailing. It will be launched at least 500 miles (800 km) above Earth. Why so high? Scientists don't want the slightest trace of atmosphere to slow it down. They will carefully track its motion for a few days to measure the thrust produced by sunlight.

HITCH *a Ride*

It is very expensive to launch a space mission. The Planetary Society could never afford to buy and fuel a rocket for LightSail-1 alone. So it will go into space as a hitchhiker on another mission where its light weight will barely be noticed.

This drawing of LightSail-1 shows the solar sail in space. Scientists are working on the technology needed to use solar sails for space missions.

IKAROS

Yuichi Tsuda, a researcher from Japan's Aerospace Exploration Agency (JAXA), displays a model of a new Japanese satellite at a press conference in Tokyo in April 2010. The satellite is called *IKAROS*, for Interplanetary Kitecraft Accelerated by Radiation of the Sun. On May 21, 2010, JAXA launched a solar sail wrapped around *IKAROS*. By June 10, *Ikaros* was 4.4 million miles (7 million km) from Earth. On that date, the sail successfully unwrapped itself.

TPS is already planning two more LightSail missions. The mission of LightSail-2 will be several months long. It will carry a few scientific instruments to make useful measurements of Earth. And it will allow scientists to improve their sailing skills. They will steer it farther from Earth like a kite riding a breeze of sunlight.

A few years after that, LightSail-3 will tackle an important job. Its mission may last for years. It will travel away from Earth toward the Sun to a point that scientists call L1. L1 is where Earth's and the Sun's gravity balance each other. L1 is 930,000 miles (1.5 million km) away from Earth, almost four times as far as the Moon.

From L1, LightSail-3 will be able to give advance warning of events on the Sun. At times, the Sun ejects large masses of electrically charged matter. The matter travels outward at a high speed. When those masses of matter strike Earth, they can disrupt communication or even cause power failures. If people have advance warning, they can avoid or reduce the damage.

After the LightSail program, the next step will be to use a solar sail to travel to another planet. TPS admits that it might take one hundred years to create the technology for high-speed sailing to the outer planets. But TPS also knows that the LightSail project is the perfect first step toward that goal.

PLASMA DRIVE ROCKETS

Remember that the exhaust from a conventional rocket propellant blasts out of the rocket nozzle at 10,000 miles (16,200 km) per hour. But suppose scientists built a rocket that could produce an exhaust speed thirty or forty times as great. The rocket would need a lot less propellant to produce the same thrust. That is the secret behind plasma drive, or ion drive, rockets.

A plasma drive gets its name from the state of matter inside of it. In everyday life, matter is a solid, a liquid, or a gas. But in all three cases, matter is made of atoms. An atom has a heavy central part called a nucleus. Surrounding the nucleus are lightweight particles called electrons.

Electricity holds atoms together. The nucleus has a positive electrical charge. Electrons are electrically negative. Positive and negative charges attract each other. But two positive charges or two negative charges push each other apart. An atom has enough negative electrons to balance the positive charge of its nucleus. That makes it electrically neutral.

It doesn't take a lot of energy to shake an electron loose from its nucleus. When that happens, the remaining negative charges don't balance the positive charge. The atom left behind is called a positive ion.

The atoms in matter are always on the move. In a gas, they often bang into one another. If a collision between atoms is very hard, it can knock away an electron and create an ion. In normal gases, most collisions don't create ions. Even when they do, the ions quickly combine with knocked-off electrons to become neutral atoms again. But when matter is very hot, the atoms bang into one another more often and with greater energy.

That creates ions faster than they can recombine with electrons. The matter is no longer made up mostly of neutral atoms. It becomes a gas of ions and electrons. That state of matter is called plasma.

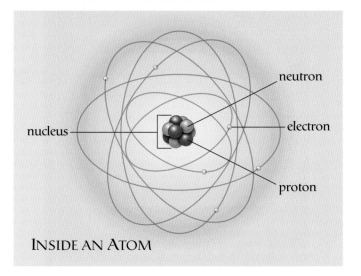

This illustration shows the electrically charged parts of an atom (electrons and protons), as well as the neutral particles called neutrons.

nucleus

neutron

electron

proton

INSIDE AN ATOM

THE FIRST ION PROPULSION ENGINE *in Space*

On October 24, 1998, NASA launched the *Deep Space 1* spacecraft on a three-year mission. Its main job was to test twelve advanced space technologies, including an ion propulsion engine. It also visited Comet Borelli and sent back some of the best images and scientific data ever from a comet.

A plasma drive is a device that supplies power to a rocket. The drive has a chamber where matter is heated to the plasma state. At one end is a nozzle where the plasma can escape. The drive also contains a very strong electric field. That field is like a giant battery with a positive end and a negative end. The positive end of the electric field pushes positive ions toward the negative end. That's where the nozzle is.

At the same time, the positive ions push back on the positive end of the field. That produces the thrust. By the time the ions reach the nozzle, they are traveling at a very high speed. They stream out of the nozzle as very high-speed exhaust. That produces a lot of thrust for a small amount of propellant.

Like solar sails, plasma drives are not powerful enough to launch a craft into space. A spacecraft will still need a conventional rocket. But once the craft is launched, plasma drives can provide a steady thrust for a long time. That can lead to very high speeds.

NASA and other space agencies plan to use plasma drive rockets in two different ways. The first is to produce the same amount of speed with less fuel. The second is to shorten the travel time for missions to other planets.

So far, space missions have used only small plasma drives to

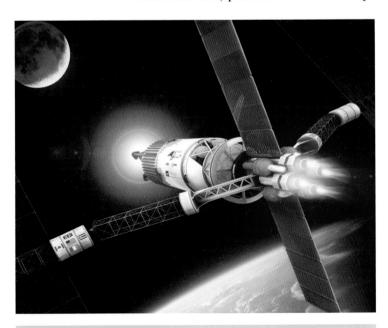

This is an artist's drawing of a proposed rocket called VASMIR. This plasma-fueled rocket could reach Mars in about a month.

*NASA's **Dawn** spacecraft uses its plasma drive engines (shown here) as it makes its way to study the asteroid Vesta.*

save weight. The best example is NASA's *Dawn*. *Dawn* is on its way to study the asteroid Vesta. Vesta is the solar system's second-largest asteroid, after Ceres. Like Ceres, Vesta orbits in the asteroid belt between Mars and Jupiter.

   Dawn was launched on September 27, 2007. Once its conventional rockets turned off, its three plasma drive engines began their slow but steady pushing. In February 2009, it got a gravity assist from Mars so it could arrive at Vesta in July 2011. *Dawn* will spend a year studying Vesta. Then the craft's plasma drive engines will start up again to launch it toward Ceres. It is expected to reach Ceres in February 2015. It will study that asteroid until July 2015.

TO THE STARS

Scientists know that as space travel becomes more common, spacecraft will need more powerful plasma drives. That's where former NASA astronaut Franklin Chang-Diaz comes in. In 2005 Chang-Diaz founded the Ad Astra Rocket Company. Ad Astra is building plasma drives for future space missions.

   Chang-Diaz has big plans for his company's products. For example, he is working to solve the issue of cosmic rays—those high-energy particles from outer space. Human travelers to Mars will be exposed to cosmic rays. Too many cosmic rays over a long period of time can damage a human body's cells.

   Ad Astra is testing plasma drive engines that would shorten the one-way trip to less than four months. And they are working on an even more powerful model that could carry astronauts from Earth to Mars in only thirty-nine days.

Astronaut Franklin Chang-Diaz is the founder of Ad Astra. That company is working to build plasma drives for missions to space. He is shown here in his NASA space suit in 1997.

That may be only the beginning. Plasma drive engines can use many different gases to create their plasma. Future space missions could use hydrogen gas. Hydrogen is very common in the universe. It can even be found in the nearly empty space between the stars.

That means a spacecraft using a hydrogen plasma-drive engine will never have to run out of fuel. It can go faster and faster until it is traveling one thousand times the speed of *New Horizons*. It could carry the first robot spacecraft to another solar system.

Chang-Diaz dreams that his company may one day build such a wonder of space technology. After all, that's why he named the company Ad Astra. That's Latin for "to the stars!"

TIMELINE

1920s Edwin Hubble discovers galaxies and the expansion of the universe. Arthur Holly Compton studies the behavior of gamma rays.

1957 The Soviet Union launches *Sputnik 1*, the first artificial satellite.

1958 The U.S. government creates the National Aeronautics and Space Administration (NASA).

1961 NASA begins its Apollo program, working on plans to send human astronauts to the Moon and return them safely.

1969 Two *Apollo 11* astronauts become the first humans to land on the Moon.

1975 The first Geostationary Operational Environmental Satellite (GOES) launches to study Earth's weather. The final Apollo mission carries U.S. astronauts to a meeting in space with Soviet cosmonauts.

1990 NASA launches the Hubble Space Telescope (HST).

1991 Space shuttle *Atlantis* carries the Compton Gamma Ray Observatory (CGRO) into orbit around Earth.

1992 Astronomers observe the first Kuiper Belt Object (KBO) other than Pluto.

1997 The *Sojourner* rover explores Mars for nearly three months.

1998 Russia launches Zarya and the United States launches Unity, the first two modules of the International Space Station (ISS). *Prospector* begins orbiting the Moon looking for hydrogen.

1999 *Columbia* carries the Chandra X-ray Observatory into Earth orbit.

2000 NASA sends Compton Gamma Ray Observatory (CGRO) into a controlled crash in the Pacific Ocean. Russia launches the ISS service module Zvezda, and the first crew arrives.

2003 The space shuttle *Columbia* breaks apart as it reenters Earth's atmosphere. NASA launches the Spitzer Space Telescope.

2004 The rovers *Spirit* and *Opportunity* land on Mars for a three-month mission.

2006 NASA launches *New Horizons* on a mission to Pluto and the Kuiper Belt.

2007 NASA launches *Dawn* to study the asteroid Vesta.

2008 The Indian Space Research Organisation (ISRO) launches *Chandrayaan-1*. The Fermi Gamma Ray Space Telescope is launched to replace CGRO.

2009 *Chandrayaan-1* detects small amounts of water everywhere on the Moon. Astronauts complete the final HST servicing mission.

2010 The final construction phase of the ISS begins. The Japanese Aerospace Exploration Agency (JAXA) launches a solar sail on the spacecraft *Ikaros*. *Voyager 1* and *Voyager 2* reach a milestone of operating continuously in space for twelve thousand days.

CHOOSE AN EIGHTH WONDER

Now that you've read about these seven wonders of space technology, do a little research to choose an eighth wonder. You may enjoy working with a friend.

You may want to start with some of the websites and books listed on pages 76 and 77. Or you may want to look at some books about the history of space travel.

When looking at a space mission, ask yourself:
- *what scientific discoveries did the mission make?*
- *what new technology made the mission special?*
- *what goals did the mission reach and what new goals followed it?*

Ad Astra!

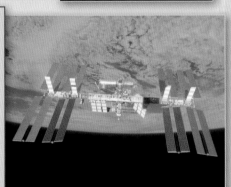

GLOSSARY

astronaut: a person who travels in space

astronomy: the study of objects and matter found in outer space

atmosphere: the gases surrounding a planet or a moon

cosmic rays: high-energy particles from outer space

electromagnetic wave: a back-and-forth pulsing of electricity and magnetism that travels through space. Light is one of many forms of electromagnetic waves.

galaxy: a system of billions of stars that travel together through space. The Sun is a star in the Milky Way Galaxy.

gamma rays: electromagnetic waves with the shortest wavelength and the highest energy

geostationary orbit: a satellite orbit around Earth's equator that takes exactly one day to complete. Because the satellite is orbiting at the same rate that Earth is turning, the satellite stays over the same point on the planet.

infrared light: a form of electromagnetic wave with wavelengths just beyond the long end of the visible light spectrum

Kuiper Belt: a region of the solar system beyond the orbit of Neptune. The belt contains many large icy bodies, including Pluto and other dwarf planets.

observatory: a telescope and the structure that surrounds it, including equipment to create images or to study the electromagnetic waves it detects

orbit: the path that a planet, a moon, or other object takes in traveling around a sun or a planet

plasma: an extremely hot state of matter made up mainly of electrons and ions rather than neutral atoms

plasma drive: an advanced rocket engine that applies a large electric field to a plasma to produce a lot of thrust from a little bit of propellant

propellant: the substance used to push a rocket. In a conventional rocket, two chemicals, a fuel and an oxidizer, burn to create that push.

rover: a vehicle designed to travel on and explore the surface of another world

solar sail: a large, lightweight reflecting structure that uses sunlight to provide a steady push to a spacecraft

solar system: a group of planets and other bodies that revolve around a star. Earth belongs to the solar system that orbits the Sun.

solar wind: a stream of high-energy electrically charged particles that comes from the Sun

space shuttle: a NASA spacecraft designed to carry human crews and equipment into orbit around Earth and to return to Earth for reuse

spectroscope: a scientific instrument that measures the spectrum (*pl.* spectra), or mixture of colors, in light

thrust: the force that a rocket engine or other system produces to increase the speed of a spacecraft

ultraviolet (UV) light: a form of electromagnetic wave with shorter wavelength than visible light

weather model: a computer program that calculates how weather conditions will change in the future

X-ray: short, high-energy electromagnetic waves

SOURCE NOTES

16 Smithsonian Astrophysical Observatory," NASA Celebrates Chandra X-ray Observatory's 10th Anniversary," Chandra X-Ray Observatory, July 23, 2009, http://chandra.harvard.edu/press/09_releases/press_072309.html (June 15, 2010).

23 Ned Potter, "Space Station Crew Reflects on NASA's Future, World Peace," ABC News.com, February 14, 2003, http://abcnews.go.com/WNT/story?id=129830 (June 15, 2010).

33 J. Marshall Shepherd, et al., "NASA's Sentinels Monitoring Weather and Climate: Past, Present, and Future," *Weatherwise*, January–February 2002.

38 Irene Klotz, "Water Found on the Moon," Discovery Channel, September 23, 2009, http://dsc.discovery.com/news/2009/09/23/moon-water.html (June 15, 2010).

41 Paul D. Spudis, "The Once and Future Moon," *Air &Space Smithsonian*, November 14, 2009, http://blogs.airspacemag.com/moon/2009/11/14/a-rainbow-on-the-moon (June 15, 2010).

47 NASA, "Mission News," *Spirit* and *Opportunity*, January 26, 2010, http://www.nasa.gov/mission_pages/mer/news/mer20100126.html (June 15, 2010).

49 Clara Ma, "Curiosity," Name NASA's Next Mars Rover, n.d., http://marsrovername.jpl.nasa.gov/WinnerAnnouncedEssay (June 15, 2010).

55 "Jupiter Flyby," *New Horizons: The First Mission to Pluto and the Kuiper Belt: Exploring Frontier Worlds*, February 2007, http://pluto.jhuapl.edu/common/content/pdfs/011607_JupiterPressKit.pdf, 5 (June 15, 2010).

58 "Launch Press Kit," *New Horizons: The First Mission to Pluto and the Kuiper Belt: Exploring Frontier Worlds*, January 2006, http://pluto.jhuapl.edu/common/content/pdfs/NHLaunchPressKit1_06.pdf, 2 (June 15, 2010).

64 Lawrence E. Lamb, *Inside the Space Race: A Space Surgeon's Diary* (Austin, TX: Synergy Books, 2006), 25.

65 Carl Sagan, quoted in Giovanni Vulpetti, Les Johnson, and Gregory L. Matloff, *Solar Sails: A Novel Approach to Interplanetary Travel* (New York: Springer, 2008), 159.

SELECTED BIBLIOGRAPHY

Bell, Jim. *Postcards from Mars: The First Photographer on the Red Planet.* New York: Dutton, 2006.

Burrows, William E. *This New Ocean: The Story of the First Space Age.* New York: Random House, 1998.

Dyson, Marianne. *Space and Astronomy: Decade by Decade.* New York: Facts on File, 2007.

Levy, David H. *Shoemaker by Levy: The Man Who Made an Impact.* Princeton, NJ: Princeton University Press, 2000.

Mooney, Chris. *Storm World: Hurricanes, Politics, and the Battle Over Global Warming.* New York: Harcourt, 2007.

Watson, Fred. *Stargazer: The Life and Times of the Telescope.* Cambridge, MA: Da Capo, 2005.

FURTHER READING AND WEBSITES

Books

Bortz, Fred. *Beyond Jupiter: The Story of Planetary Astronomer Heidi Hammel.* Danbury, CT: Franklin Watts, 2005. Be on the scene with Heidi Hammel and other planetary astronomers as the *Voyager 2* spacecraft sends back images of Uranus and Neptune. Also share Hammel's best-known discoveries from Hubble Space Telescope, including images of the impacts of pieces of Comet Shoemaker-Levy 9 with Jupiter.

Butts, Ellen R., and Joyce R. Schwartz. *Carl Sagan.* This biography of American astronomer and author Carl Sagan looks at his lifelong quest for answers to questions about outer space and our place in the universe.

Johnson, Rebecca L. *Satellites.* Minneapolis: Lerner Publishing Company, 2006. Part of the Cool Science series, this book discusses the history, development, and uses of artificial satellites.

Kuhn, Betsy. *The Race for Space: The United States and the Soviet Union Compete for the New Frontier.* Minneapolis: Twenty-First Century Books, 2007. Feel the excitement of the international competition to put humans on the Moon.

Miller, Ron. *Stars and Galaxies.* Minneapolis: Twenty-First Century Books, 2006. Part of the Worlds Beyond series, *Stars and Galaxies* looks at the amazing star systems that fill the universe. Other books in the series include *Asteroids, Comets, and Meteors, Earth and the Moon, Extrasolar Planets, The Sun,* and books for each planet.

Silverstein, Alvin, Virginia Silverstein, and Laura Silverstein Nunn. *Weather and Climate.* Minneapolis: Twenty-First Century Books, 1998. This book examines the changes in the atmosphere that produce various weather phenomena and how weather patterns over a period of time determine the climates of Earth's various regions.

Siy, Alexandra. *Cars on Mars: Roving the Red Planet.* Watertown, MA: Charlesbridge, 2009. Discover the story of *Spirit* and *Opportunity* from liftoff through their first five years of roving the Red Planet in this book filled with dramatic pictures from the twin rovers' remarkable missions.

Stott, Carole. *Mission: Space.* New York: DK, 2008. Full-color photos and charts highlight this tour of our galaxy and the technology used to study it.

Ward, D. J. *Exploring Mars.* Minneapolis: Lerner Publications Company, 2007. Journey to the Red Planet with probes and rovers.

Websites

ESA Kids
http://www.esa.int/esaKIDSen
This European Space Agency website features information on past and current missions, life in space, weather satellites, and the story of the universe.

Hubble Site
http://hubblesite.org
The official Hubble website explains the construction, workings, and the mission of the HST. The site also contains a gallery of Hubble images (planets, nebulas, stars, and more), an interactive map for locating the HST in orbit, and a section on exploring astronomy.

International Space Station
http://www.nasa.gov/mission_pages/station/main/index.html
This NASA website features photos, videos, behind-the-scenes stories, and the latest ISS news.

NASA Education
http://www.nasa.gov/audience/forstudents/index.html
NASA's website for students includes interactive features, research and homework tools, podcasts, photos, and much more.

NOAA Education: Cool Sites for Everyone
http://www.education.noaa.gov/coolsites.html
Learn about weather satellites, weather models, climate change, and more!

INDEX

ABOUT THE AUTHOR

Fred Bortz is a scientist and a writer of science and technology for young people. In his books, articles, and personal appearances, he shares with his audience the joy of discovery that fueled his previous twenty-five-year career in teaching and research in physics, engineering, and science education. He earned his doctorate in physics in 1971 from Carnegie Mellon University, where he was involved in research from 1979 through 1994. He is also a regular reviewer of science books for several major metropolitan newspapers.

PHOTO ACKNOWLEDGMENTS

The images in this book are used with the permission of: NASA, pp. 5, 11, 20, 21, 22, 24, 27, 35, 37, 45, 71, 73 (right center); © Babak Tafreshi/Photo Researchers, Inc., p. 6; © Brian Grant/Dreamstime.com, p. 7; Mary Evans Picture Library/Everett Collection, p. 8; © Laura Westlund/Independent Picture Service, pp. 9, 68; © Margaret Bourke-White/Time & Life Pictures/Getty Images, p. 10; NASA/JPL, pp. 12, 18, 42, 43, 51, 70; NASA/JSC, pp. 13, 23; NASA/KSC, p. 15; NASA/CXC/M. Weiss, p. 17; NASA/JPL-Caltech/K.Su (Univ. of Ariz.), p. 19; ESA-AOES Medialab, pp. 28, 73 (bottom center); © Tctomm/Dreamstime.com, p. 29; © Scientifica/Visuals Unlimited, Inc., p. 30; NASA/Tom Farrar, Sandy Joseph, p. 32; © Gunnar Kulenberg/SuperStock, p. 34; NASA/ARC, p. 39; ISRO/NASA/JPL-Caltech/Brown Univ./USGS, p. 40; © World History Archive/Alamy, p. 44; NASA/JPL-Caltech, pp. 46, 49, 73 (top center); Mars Exploration Rover Mission, Cornell, JPL, NASA, p. 47; NASA/JHUAPL/SwRI, pp. 50, 57, 59, 73 (bottom right); © Friedrich Saurer/Alamy, p. 52; NASA/Kim Shiftlett, p. 54; NASA/Bill Ingalls, p. 60; NASA/1-Meter Schmidt Telescope/ESO, p. 61; T. Abott and NOAO/AURA/NSF, p. 62; © Classic Image/Alamy, p. 64; Planetary Society, p. 66; © YOSHIKAZU TSUNO/AFP/Getty Images, p. 67; © Ad Astra Rocket Company, p. 69; David Imbaratto, Stellar Exploration, for the Planetary Society, p. 73 (top left); © Stocktrek Images/Getty Images, 73 (top right); NASA/Honeywell Tech Solutions, C. Meaney, p. 73 (bottom left).

Front cover: © Stocktrek Images/Getty Images (top left); ESA - AOES Medialab (top center); David Imbaratto, Stellar Exploration, for the Planetary Society (top right); NASA (center); NASA/Honeywell Tech Solutions, C. Meaney (bottom left); NASA/JPL-Caltech (bottom middle); NASA/JHUAPL/SwRI (bottom right).